TARRY FLYNN

Peter Fallon

TARRY FLYNN

A play in Three Acts
based on the novel
by Patrick Kavanagh

for Emma,
with all good wishes,

Peter Fallon

Gallery Books

Tarry Flynn
is first published
simultaneously in paperback
and in a clothbound edition
on the day of its première,
10 September 2004.

The Gallery Press
Loughcrew
Oldcastle
County Meath
Ireland

ISBN 1 85235 376 7 (*paperback*)
     1 85235 377 5 (*clothbound*)

A CIP catalogue record for this book
is available from the British Library.

Patrick and Katherine Kavanagh
on their wedding day,
Dublin, 19 April 1967

Characters

in order of appearance
CHARLIE TRAINOR, calf-dealer, 30*
HUGHIE COYLE, late 20s
TARRY FLYNN, late 20s
EUSEBIUS CASSIDY, late 20s, but younger than Tarry
MRS FLYNN, a widow, Tarry's mother
BRIDIE, nearly 30
AGGIE, 21
FR MARKEY, curate of Dargan
MARY REILLY, 18
PATSY MEEGAN, 60s
TOMMY QUINN, early 20s
UNCLE PETEY

*Looks a little more well-to-do than Hughie and Tarry and Eusebius. Newer suit, shined shoes? His work takes him further afield.

Time and Place

The townland of Drumnay, in Dargan, County Cavan, Ireland. The Feast of Corpus Christi, 1935, and the weeks afterwards.

Tarry Flynn by Peter Fallon, based on the novel by Patrick Kavanagh, was first produced by the Selkie Theatre Company at The Ice House in Bethlehem, PA, on Friday, 10 September 2004, with the following cast:

CHARLIE TRAINOR	Kevin Winter-Deely
HUGHIE COYLE	Graham P Stanford
TARRY FLYNN	Patrick Kelly
EUSEBIUS CASSIDY	Peter Sanchez
MRS FLYNN	Sharon McGinnis
BRIDIE	Jean Sidden
AGGIE	Rebecca Levine
FR MARKEY	Whitt Brantley
MARY REILLY	Madeline T Hoak
PATSY MEEGAN	Dan Sigley
TOMMY QUINN	Aaron Coyle
UNCLE PETEY	Steve Hatzai

Director	George B Miller
Producers	Kate Scuffle and George B Miller
Design	Jeff Reidy and Michael Schofield
Original Music	L E McCullough
Dialect Consultant	Yvonne Molloy

to the memories of

Katherine B Kavanagh
(1928-1989)

and my uncle
Peter Mullan
(1913-1983)

PROLOGUE

Begin: Air of 'The Dawning of the Day' quietly melting into late spring/early summer's evening, near dark.

CHARLIE TRAINOR, HUGHIE COYLE, TARRY FLYNN and EUSEBIUS CASSIDY are sitting near a gate by the ditch on the side of Drumnay lane, where it joins the main road. Smoking, probably. First see the lights from their cigarettes and their various outlines/silhouettes. They are passing the time as they obviously do many evenings. The scene is stylized. It should move formally at first and then, after concluding exchange and TARRY's outburst, seem to end abruptly, as if frozen. TARRY's other-ness should be established: he can stand aside, look only half-interested etc.

CHARLIE   (*Continuing; his turn*) So your man walks into the butcher's shop and says he to your man, Have you a pig's head? And the butcher says, Wha'? I said, Have you a pig's head? And the butcher says, No, it's just the way I comb me hair.

> *The others, except TARRY, gesture their acknowledgement, approving.*

Isn't that a good one, wha'?

HUGHIE   It's a good one alright.

> *No response from TARRY.*

I never heard better.

CHARLIE   What do you think, Tarry?

TARRY   (*Without conviction*) Great. Great. It's a great one.

CHARLIE   (*Thrilled with himself*) It's just the way I comb me hair!

11

EUSEBIUS Listen. (*He has told this before, and most of them have heard it before, but that stops nothing*) We'd an old clock in our house once — Father bought it second-hand for half-a-crown thirty years earlier, and the old woman *he* bought it from had herself bought it second-hand forty years earlier still. (*Rehearsed, as if he's remembering something and is reciting it*) That clock was as touchy as a spoiled child; it would only go for Father. Not even Jock Brickle could make it keep time. Once indeed, Father did let Jock try his hand at the old time-piece. He took it asunder, and when he put it back together there was one wheel for which the clock repairer could find no place. He tried to fix that wheel in sideways, anglewise, backwise, and while he was at it, the old clock started *Tick-tock, tick-tock.*

'There's a wheel too many in your clock,' says Jock.

HUGHIE Wha'? What was that, Eusebius?

EUSEBIUS He said, There was a wheel too many in your clock.

HUGHIE Oh, that's a good one, a right good one.

CHARLIE What do you think, Tarry?

TARRY (*Withering*) It was always a good one.

Pause.

CHARLIE Did you hear anything about the other thing, Tarry — no developments?

TARRY Heard she went to the Big Man about it.

CHARLIE Holy God! To Father Markey?

HUGHIE She was seen going up to the Parochial.

EUSEBIUS (*Relishing*) There'll be sport about this, there'll be sport alright.

TARRY (*Abruptly*) They can all go to Hell!

Hold. Return to outlines/silhouettes. Their passing the time continues.

ACT ONE

Scene One

Early morning. Feast of Corpus Christi. Kitchen of Flynns' relatively comfortable farmhouse. Lights up on TARRY *standing on a stool searching on the top of the dresser.*

MRS FLYNN *sits barefoot by the fire with her shoes on the floor beside her, fondling a corn on her little toe. Her husband has died some years previously. All she says modulates between rage/exasperation and a restrained wish to love. She knows no way to express this feeling. She has worked too hard. She has been too hurt. Her outbursts of rage should rise and fall, rise and fall, like the tide. She is desperately conscious of her — and her family's — place in the eyes of the world. Though he breaks her heart, she dotes on* TARRY.

TARRY Where the devil did I put me cap? (*To nobody in particular*) Did any of ye see me cap?

> *He lifts an old schoolbook lying in the dust of the dresser-top and takes a quick glance at the tattered pages. Then, after a while, to himself, clearly*

God is in the bits and pieces of every day.

MRS FLYNN (*Not hearing, because she doesn't understand*) What in the name of the devil's father are you looking for at such an hour in the morning? Are you going to go to Mass at all? (*She swings around*) Looking on top of the dresser! Mind you don't put the big awkward hooves on that tray of eggs that's under you.

TARRY A fine bloody place to lave (*leave*) them.

MRS FLYNN They'll make more money nor you anyway.

> *Pause. Kitchen activity, tidying, brushing the fire-*

place with a goose's wing, fussing.

(*Quieter*) What was that you said about God and the —

TARRY   I said, God is in the bits and pieces of every day.

MRS FLYNN   Lord protect everyone's rearing. The things you do say about religion and the priests.

Pause.

(*Starting up again*) Well of all the mane (*mean*) men that ever was, you're the manest. Of a holy-day morning to be looking for the oul' cap at twenty-five past eight. Anything to be late for Mass. And if it wasn't the cap it'd be something else — the stud, or there'd be a button off the coat. Just like your Uncle Petey that never gave himself more nor five minutes to walk to Mass. He'd keep looking at himself in the looking glass till, honest to God, it'd make you sick to see him.

TARRY   (*He's heard it all before*) Ah, don't be bothering me.

MRS FLYNN   That's your Uncle Petey all over. Nobody could talk to him; he knew it all and everything. He'd take on to put a leg on a horse — and the whole country laughing at him.

Will you get down to hell out of that and go to Mass! On the blessèd day of Corpus Christi to think of a man sling-slanging about the house and first Mass near half-over.

TARRY   Amn't I taking the bicycle?

MRS FLYNN   (*Reciting her litany of woes*) Hens not fed, the pot not on for the pigs — and you washed in the well water!

Pause. MRS FLYNN *sticks her feet in her shoes. She stands up and looks out the window.*

Where's this one?

BRIDIE   (*Entering from upstairs, with a bucket*) I'm here.

MRS FLYNN   Lord God of Almighty, but you're another of the

Sunday girls. Lying up there in bed like a churn a-drying. Have you no shame at all? If it's not this man here it's one of yous. That's what left the Carlins where they are — getting up, one at eight and the other at nine, making two breakfasts. If they had one breakfast now they wouldn't be as hard to talk to.

MRS FLYNN *looks out the window again. She likes to keep an eye on things.*

Ours was a united house. There was only one purse, let it be full or empty. One purse, and one breakfast. There, it's half-eight now and no sign of you (TARRY) going.

TARRY Haven't I bags of time? Bags of it. Don't I know right well you put that clock on half an hour last night?

BRIDIE *goes to the door, glances up and down, rushes out, and returns with the bucket empty.*

BRIDIE (*Yawning, stretching*) A terrible close morning.
MRS FLYNN Did you look to see if the hen in the barrel broke any of the eggs?
BRIDIE None, so far as I could see.
MRS FLYNN I wouldn't put it past you but you didn't look at all. Will you try and get this fellow his cap and get him away to Mass — the oul' haythen.

TARRY, *sitting on the side of the table, starts fumbling with a cigarette.*

Lord! Lord! Lord! Starting to puff at the curse-o'-God fag at such an hour of the morning.

BRIDIE *lifts an old newspaper on the window sill.*

BRIDIE There's the oul' cap. He must be blind that he

couldn't get it.

MRS FLYNN Didn't want to get it. Will you like a decent girl run out to the cart-house and see if his bicycle's pumped?

BRIDIE It's hard enough. It'll carry him.

MRS FLYNN A poor thing. A poor thing to rear a man that doesn't care for God, man or the devil. And him knowing full well that I have to go to the market this day with them cocks that we caught last night. I hope I'll be able to swap them for pullets.

Lord! Oh Lord! He should have left here to go to Mass at five minutes to eight and there's that man still steaming away like a railway engine. Take Carroll's factory to keep him in fags. (*To* BRIDIE) Go up the loft steps and see if you can see Aggie coming with the milk. We haven't a drop for the breakfast.

AGGIE *passes the window and enters with a can of milk which she puts down on the floor.*

AGGIE I see the strawberry's looking the bull. She didn't give me half as much as she ought to.

MRS FLYNN (*Making a mental calculation*) She couldn't be looking the bull, I don't think. She took the bull a fortnight ago. (*Pause*) We'll have to sell her a stripper if she doesn't keep the bull. Be a terrible loss if she won't keep the bull.

AGGIE The white cow has a tear on her teat that's a total dread — like a tear from a buck wire.

MRS FLYNN Oh, that's more of this man's doing. How many times did I tell him to fix that paling and not to have the wire trailing halfway across the field. To look at the place a person would think we hadn't a man about it.

Oh, look at him there with his big nose and the oul' cod of a face like his Uncle Petey that — that a Protestant wouldn't be worse than him!

BRIDIE (*Who has been waiting for this moment*) And there's more than that, the dirty oul' dog. (*She has attracted and is holding* MRS FLYNN's *attention.* AGGIE *gets interested, too*) There's other things going on worse nor that, things that might get us all into trouble.

MRS FLYNN (*Trying not to be concerned*) Arra, what?

BRIDIE (*Enjoying this, teasing*) If some fellows we know are not in jail before the next week or so it'll be surprising.

MRS FLYNN God, Oh God! Oh God! Is it something to do with this fella here?

BRIDIE A girl knocked off her bicycle at Drumnay Cross —

AGGIE (*Who knows all about it, too*) And there's going to be trouble about it.

MRS FLYNN Was heavy hands laid on some poor girl? And who was she?

BRIDIE Mary Reilly.

BRIDIE *looks at* TARRY.

AGGIE Whatever was done to her we don't know only what we heard.

TARRY (*Trying to be dismissive*) It's all nonsense.

MRS FLYNN (*Off again*) Isn't it a poor thing that I can't have one day's peace with the whole rick-ma-tick of yous? (*Sitting down*) I won't be the better of this for a week. (*Rallying; to* BRIDIE) Go and strain that milk before you feed the hens.

BRIDIE (*To* AGGIE) Come on, you.

BRIDIE *and* AGGIE *exit.*

MRS FLYNN (*To* TARRY) And what have you done to the girl?

TARRY Nothing. (*Uncomfortable, awkward in the accusation*) Nothing, nothing at all.

MRS FLYNN There has to be something — or those two wouldn't have it. Lord, Oh Lord! Why can't you be like another, and not have us all the talk of the country?
   Not that I care a straw for that whipster of Reilly's — a stuck-up thing that — a bit of a mauling wouldn't do her much harm. But you to get your

17

name up with it, that's what I can't stand. It's a pity you wouldn't try to keep away from that Cross. Get up now and go to Mass and be back quick in case you have to go to Kerley's with that cow. Go and pray and confess your sins and you'll have all the luck.

TARRY *goes out. She watches him, her heart bursting with a love she can't express.*

(*Quietly, almost to herself*) Forever reading and dreaming to himself in the field. My heart was often in my mouth that he'd turn the cart upside down in a gripe while he was dreaming or looking at the flowers.

She enters her own reverie — scene ends slowly.

Scene Two

At the door/back of the Dargan Parish Church. Porch? Foot of the balcony steps, perhaps? Priest doesn't need to be seen: could be heard from inside. We need to see three or four men kneeling/slouching etc. including CHARLIE, HUGHIE *and* EUSEBIUS, *with* TARRY *standing aside, taking off bicycle clips, straightening hair, clothes, etc.*

EUSEBIUS   Damn nice morning.

TARRY   A terror.

EUSEBIUS   Well?

TARRY   Damn the thing doing, Eusebius.

EUSEBIUS   Be jaybers! (*Quieter*) Did you see her?

TARRY   I did. (*Important*) She has no fella as far as I know.

EUSEBIUS   I often thought I could get going with her, you know — if I went all-out.

TARRY   I was thinking you'd a notion of her.

EUSEBIUS   (*Afraid to admit it*) What put that into your head? I wouldn't walk the side of the road that she'd be on.

TARRY   I seen Tom on the job again.

EUSEBIUS   Aye, the oul' clown. Some people wouldn't know when they were insulted. (*Gestures at* HUGHIE, *making sure he's out of earshot*) Hughie Coyle tried his hardest for Josie Duffy and he might as well be idle.

TARRY   No Go for Hughie.

EUSEBIUS   (*Looking aside*) That's like your mother.

> *Their chat stops suddenly. They join the edges of the congregation.*

CHARLIE   Very weedy piece of spuds, them of Joe Finnegan's.

HUGHIE   He doesn't put on the dung, Charlie: the man that doesn't drive on the dung won't take out a crop. (*Pause*) Nothing like the dung.

CHARLIE   Give me your cap till I kneel on it.

HUGHIE   All the kneeling you'll do —

> TARRY *moves closer. Suggest drone of ceremony, hum*

of prayer.

EUSEBIUS He couldn't see the women from here.

The others laugh, nudge each other.

FR MARKEY (*Loud, as if from on high, long pauses throughout, loud blow of nose before he begins*) There was a great poet one time, and his name was Tom Moore. He wrote a song called 'Rich and Rare'.
Rich and rare were the gems she wore . . .

Blows nose again, then solemn, enunciating every word separately.

Rich and rare were the gems she wore
And a bright gold ring on her hand she bore;
But O her beauty was far beyond
Her sparkling gem and snow-white wand.

Lady, dost thou not fear to stray
So lone and lovely on this bleak way?
Sir Knight, I fear not the least alarm,
No son of Erin would offer me harm.

Pause.

That couldn't be said of a lady passing through the village or Parish of Dargan today. (*Sighing*) No, it could not. (*Raised voice*) Rapscallions of hell, curmudgeons of the devil that are less civilized than the natives on the banks of the Congo.

Everyone leans forward, delighted with the sermon.
CHARLIE *peeps though a chink in the woodwork.*

EUSEBIUS Come to hell outa that, or he'll see you.
CHARLIE Everything's game ball. (*Winks*)
FR MARKEY Hypocrites, humbugs, coming here Sunday after

Sunday — blindfolding the devil in the dark, as the saying goes. And the headquarters of all this rascality is a townland called Drumnay. (*Everybody, including* TARRY, *smiles, as* FR MARKEY *stoops his head [if we see him], or changes his tone sorrowfully*) A young girl was passing through this village the other evening. She was riding her bicycle home from Confession. When she was passing Drumnay crossroads she was set upon by a crowd of blackguards — and blackguards is no name for them — and the clothes tore off her back. Good God. Good God, what is this country coming to?

(*Relaxing passion, more softly*) I don't blame the unfortunate wretches so much, but I do blame the half-educated blackguards who put them up to such work — the men who make the balls for others to fire, oh, they're the blackguards, the men who pick the stones for others to throw.

EUSEBIUS *and* TARRY *exchange winks and a nod.*

I'll not rest or relax till I make an example of these scoundrels who are sullying the fair name of this parish. I'll bring them to the bar of justice if it takes me years. Yes, Drumnay crossroads, where a decent man or woman can't pass without a clod being thrown at them or some nasty expression. They come here to Mass and they were better at home — a thousand times better.

He breaks off suddenly and turns to other announcements. Shuffling and stretching in the congregation.

A grand carnival dance will be held in the hall this evening. Gentlemen — two-and-six; Ladies — two shillings. The right of admission will be strictly reserved —

Trails off, fades.

Scene Three

Kitchen. Tea-time. MRS FLYNN *busy.* BRIDIE *and* AGGIE *at the mirror, making themselves up.*

MRS FLYNN (*Chastising*) The devil thank ye and thump ye, Bridie. Your face is scrubbed often enough and the damn to the much you're making of it. I could be twice married when I was your age.

BRIDIE (*Giving as good as she's getting*) A wonder you didn't make a better bargain then.

MRS FLYNN Arra what? Are you making little of your poor father — the Lord have mercy on him.

BRIDIE (*Giving up*) Oh nobody can talk to you. If a person only opens their mouth ye ait the face off them.

MRS FLYNN Oh a family of daughters is the last of the last. Half the time painting and powdering and it would take a doctor's shop to keep them in medicine. Go out, one of yes, and bring in a lock of sticks.

Neither reacts. TARRY *enters from the field.*

(*To* TARRY) You were born at mealtime. I didn't expect you home a while. Did you get finished?

TARRY I did.

He sits down and starts flicking through The Messenger.

MRS FLYNN (*To the daughters*) There's that poor fella there and he didn't get a drop of tay and him tired working in the field all day. Go now and put on the kettle, Bridie, and make his tay.

BRIDIE He'll die, poor chap, if he doesn't get his tay.

AGGIE Nothing for the mother only the big fella.

TARRY *begins to revel in the attention.*

BRIDIE   (*Impatient*) And he's as lazy. As lazy —

AGGIE   (*Almost aside*) He's like Con Kearney's oul' bitch that had to lean against the wall to bark.

BRIDIE   There's no talk of making tay for us when we come in —

AGGIE   And we're doing more than him.

MRS FLYNN   What are yes doing? What are yes doing? I don't see much of your work.

> *Sisters give up; they start getting tea.* MRS FLYNN *goes over to* TARRY, *softening.*

How did you get on the day, Tarry?

TARRY   Nearly finished.

MRS FLYNN   Ye shouldn't try to do a bull-dragging day. Isn't there more days nor years? (*Suddenly*) Listen. Listen.

> *She moves towards the door.*

I hope to the sweet honourable Father that it's not someone coming in on top of us at this hour of the evening. Whip that kettle off the fire, Aggie, and not have us making tay.

> *Suddenly there's a conspiratorial rush to put things in order. Angers have melted.* AGGIE *shoves the kettle under the stairs (or table).* BRIDIE *disarranges the clean mugs, etc. It becomes apparent no one is coming. The relief allows* AGGIE *and* BRIDIE *to re-enact a scene. This practice of mimicking recurs in the play and has the effect of amusing and uniting the family.*

AGGIE   Do you mind this morning? Mrs Tallon came dandering by, and says she (*she gestures to her mother; then, as Mrs Flynn, ever so sweet*) Won't you come in an' rest your stockings, Mrs Tallon?

BRIDIE   (*As Mrs Tallon, pathetic whinge*) I can't till I get me ducks. Would you let me look into your stable to see if they might be there, Mrs Flynn? I thought I saw them coming this way.

AGGIE (*As Mrs Flynn, grand*) Troth, the only time, Mrs Tallon, that you'd be sure of finding your ducks about our street is when we're feeding the hens. They're the boys for eating our hens' feeding, Mrs Tallon (*she stresses each 'Mrs Tallon'*), but as for dropping an egg here, Mrs Tallon, that's the last thing they'd think of.

MRS FLYNN *is enjoying this now.*

(*Exaggerating even more*) Oh, catch them to lay about a stranger's place.

MRS FLYNN (*Interrupting*) That party never fed man nor baste in their whole life.

AGGIE (*Continuing, as Mrs Flynn, sweetly*) Tarry, did you chance to see Mrs Tallon's ducks knocking about today?

The whole family has become involved in the play-acting — this is, after all, a family which unites against anyone else — TARRY *laughing and blushing simultaneously.*

BRIDIE (*As Tarry, now, greatly exaggerated*) They were over in our field trying to find worms in the drills a couple or three hours ago. After that I seen them making for Cassidys' field of oats.

MRS FLYNN Mane lot of beggars and the concait of them. Why that young whipster of theirs, May, you'd think she was the lady of the land.

TARRY *looks interested first, then wounded. All references to girls attract his interest.*

Shh. Listen. (*At window*) Is that Patsy Meegan I see? Another slack gelding. The devil the women he'll ever take now. An ould man thinking about young girls is the worst of the worst. What kind of oats are you going to sow when that happens?

They settle into quieter routines.

(*Re-establishing the hierarchy of the household, to the daughters*) Go out, one of yes, I said, and bring in a lock of sticks.

> BRIDIE *and* AGGIE *look at each other and leave quietly.* MRS FLYNN *and* TARRY *alone in a gentler atmosphere.* TARRY *continues reading; then, suddenly, to no one in particular*

TARRY The Holy Spirit is in the fields.
MRS FLYNN (*She has heard, but doesn't respond. Again, she doesn't understand*) There's a curse o' God corn on that wee toe and it's starting to bother me again. I think we'll have a slash of rain. Get the razor blade and pare it for me.

> TARRY *takes her foot between his legs like a black-smith shoeing a horse.*

Easy now, and don't draw blood. Easy now.

Pause.

What was that you said about the Holy something?
TARRY I said, The Holy Spirit is in the fields.
MRS FLYNN (*Puzzling*) Is it something to do with the Catholic religion you mean?
TARRY It has to do with every religion; it's beauty in nature.

> MRS FLYNN *throws up her eyes, half amused, half terrified.*

MRS FLYNN At least there was no madness on my side of the house. (*Then, remembering*) The Mission's opening next Sunday, I hear. I hope this'll stir up the pack of good-for-nothings that's on the go in Dargan. And you'll have to be there, too.

Pause.

TARRY (*Who has obviously given the matter some thought*) I believe that the two men that's coming are the two toughest men in the Order.

MRS FLYNN It might indeed stir them up. I was talking to one of the McArdles there and I was telling him that he ought to be getting a woman. 'Huh,' says he, 'what would I be doing with a woman? Haven't I me pint and me fag?'

You'll have to go the Mission every evening, Tarry. I don't want to have the people talking, and it's talking they'd be. The last time there was a Mission in this parish — How many years ago would that be? It's either ten or eleven — the devil a go the Carlins ever went and their luck was never the better of it. Oh, they had the devil's luck ever since.

BRIDIE *and* AGGIE *return, with the firewood.*

I mind it well, the last Mission, whenever it was. Men who had forgotten what they were born for came out from Confession ready to bull cows. Or that's the way Charlie Trainor had it.

They all laugh at this. TARRY *gets up to go out.*

You made a great job of that corn, Tarry. I hadn't a foot to put under me.

TARRY *leaves.* MRS FLYNN *relaxes a moment. Then* TARRY *re-enters.*

Are you back?

TARRY I thought I left something here.

He starts rooting around.

BRIDIE Don't be throwing *The Messenger* on the ground and me not having it read.

TARRY Sure there's nothing in it — only rubbish.

AGGIE That's the class of a man Tarry is. Always making little of religion.

MRS FLYNN For God's sake, don't let anyone outside hear you saying these things. The people that's going in this place are only waiting for the chance to carry stories to the Parochial House — like what happened the Reilly one.

> TARRY *hesitates at this, then busies himself, rummaging.*

(*To* TARRY) What in the name of the Lord are you pooching for?

TARRY For nothing, I tell you.

MRS FLYNN (*Realizes*) There's a shilling there on the dresser and you can take it. But try and not spend it. You're soft enough with other people's money. I like a man to have money in his pocket.

> TARRY *takes the money, and goes out singing.*

Scene Four

A few days later. Outside on the lane. MARY *is wheeling a bicycle when she comes alongside* TARRY *fiddling with/fixing a knapsack sprayer. He looks into the hedge and the field as if he's lost something. But he is aware of her presence. As he turns, he rubs his chin: he should have shaved. Note: the light in both scenes featuring* TARRY *with* MARY *should be different, luminous. And* TARRY *should be more animated.*

TARRY Hello.
MARY Hello.

> TARRY *can hardly believe the sweetness of her reply. Again, little is said. Looks tell plenty.* TARRY *talks nervously. She listens, enthralled.*

TARRY Is the bicycle flat?
MARY No.

> TARRY'S *look says, Then why were you walking? and dares believe the reason. He looks down, embarrassed at his working clothes, patched trousers.*

TARRY She's a terrible woman for keeping oul' trousers on the go.

> MARY *longs for the words to put him at ease.*

MARY I often saw worse around our place. On the men. (*She means the workmen. Noticing* TARRY *is stung, she would like to retract the inference*) That's not what I meant.
TARRY (*Fumbling*) Great weather.
MARY Fierce.
TARRY (*Looking all around, and up*) Did you ever see clearer skies?
MARY Never. I never did.

28

Awkward silence.

TARRY I want to tell you something —
MARY What?
TARRY I think I could say it to you, because you're different —
MARY (*Embarrassed*) You'd be surprised.
TARRY Oh God. (*He can't go on. He goes on*) It wasn't me. It wasn't —
MARY What? What are you saying?
TARRY The other night.
MARY What?
TARRY Above at the Cross.

> MARY *shrinks from the thought.*

    Honest to God. That's the last thing I'd think of doing!
MARY (*Slowly*) I know that.

> *The mood lightens. A load is lifted from* TARRY, *though he can't let the subject go.*

TARRY It wouldn't be past Eusebius though, for all his talk.
MARY (*Because of her kindness*) I don't know about that.

> TARRY, *apprehending that ice has been broken, dares*

TARRY Will you come down this way some evening till we have a talk? (*Afraid he has been too bold*) I was only joking.
MARY (*Knows what he's trying to say and answers quickly, keenly*) I will.
TARRY (*Caught off guard*) You wha'?
MARY I will.
TARRY You will not!
MARY Isn't that what you want?
TARRY Me? Want? (*Disbelieving it could be true*) Sure I was

only acting the cod!

MARY (*Directly*) Well if you want me to, it's what I want too.

TARRY *You* want?

MARY (*Ill at ease*) Well, it was your idea.

TARRY (*Recovering*) Of course I want, it's just —

MARY Just what?

> TARRY *looks at his clothes, rubs his chin, weighs his world.*

(*Continues*) What about Thursday evening?

TARRY (*Still flustered*) Oh, not at all, not at all.

> MARY *laughs. He tries to laugh, too.*

MARY So it's Thursday?

TARRY Thursday.

MARY (*Knowing she must lead, he's too confused*) About eight o'clock?

TARRY Eight? That's awful early. How would I have all the work done and the dinner ate and —

MARY (*Amused*) Well, what about nine?

TARRY Nine! That's awful late. (*Knowing the ridiculousness of it all*) No, no, no, nine'd be fine. Fine. Eight. Eight'd be perfect. (*He can hardly believe it*)

MARY Right so. I'll see you on Thursday. (*She begins to move off*) At nine.

TARRY What?

MARY I'm only joking. At eight o'clock.

> *As she wheels her bicycle off, she looks back, and smiles.*

TARRY (*Enthralled*) Please God she'll mind herself. (*Then, returning to the actuality, groans*) You didn't say you were 'only acting the cod' and 'Not at all'. You said (*gently*) Yes — dear — Thursday evening at eight will be — wonderful.

He stares into the audience.

I'm the two ends of a gulpin.

He kicks the ditch, curses himself and everything.
Lights down quickly. Lights up slowly on next scene,
which is a continuation and could be joined.

Scene Five

TARRY hears somebody coming, recovers. Then he readies himself to put on the sprayer. EUSEBIUS enters, with the usual spring in his step. EUSEBIUS has seen the end of what's just passed, but isn't quite sure how to address it.

EUSEBIUS The hard man!
TARRY There you are. How's things?
EUSEBIUS The best. The best. Never better.

> *They settle into idle talk.*

TARRY Blowy weather.
EUSEBIUS It's brave and cool, alright.
TARRY (*Hesitant still and conscious of 'Mary' encounter*) No rain a while yet.

> EUSEBIUS *keeps looking in the direction* MARY *departed, to keep the episode alive.*

EUSEBIUS These turnips could be doing with a sup soon. You know, you ought to hurry with the praties before the ground gets too dry.
TARRY I put clay up to those spuds the other day and they're doing terrible well.
EUSEBIUS The potash is your man.
TARRY (*Defensively*) I only put on the bare hundred.
EUSEBIUS (*Hinting he knows better*) You did, and the rest.

> *Pause. Then, out of nowhere, with a sense of urgent necessity.*

TARRY I'm going to ask you a thing I often had a mind to ask you before.
EUSEBIUS (*Feigning indifference*) Yeah?
TARRY And who else could I ask, only yourself?
EUSEBIUS I know. Go on. Say the piece.

TARRY   Had you ever anything to do with a woman, Eusebius?

EUSEBIUS   (*Taken aback and disarmed*) Good God, God, no!

TARRY   Can I take that for the God's honest truth?

EUSEBIUS   (*Embarrassed, stumbling*) You can surely. To be sure. Sure.

> TARRY *is relieved.* EUSEBIUS *wants to change the subject.*

You know I took a run round Duffys' the other night.

> TARRY *is interested.*

Just for a cod, you understand. And do you know I never saw such a house, shining like a kitten's eye — plates stacked on the dresser and everything. Hell of a crowd in there drinking tay and porter. It's a dread.

TARRY   Many of the younger ones about?

EUSEBIUS   Only Anne.

TARRY   (*Half to himself*) Oh God. (*Shifts tone, trying to reveal his concern*) Would you say the young ones are still alright?

EUSEBIUS   What do you think?

TARRY   (*Struggling*) It'd be hard to say — for sure, you know —

EUSEBIUS   All women's as bad as the Duffys if they get the chance.

> *Pause.* TARRY *absorbs* EUSEBIUS's *condemnation.*

TARRY   I'd my eye on the two younger ones for years and was only waiting for them to get big enough.

EUSEBIUS   You — and half the parish.

TARRY   Are you sure about that?

EUSEBIUS   I'm as sure as there's an eye in a hawk.

> EUSEBIUS *warms to* TARRY's *discomfort.*

I was crossing the railway the other night and who did I meet only Josie. Says she, 'Are you coming down the line?'

TARRY Josie Duffy! The one with the children?

EUSEBIUS The very one. 'Good God, no,' says I (*relishing this,* TARRY *all ears*), 'I'm late for the Mission as I am!'

> TARRY *is deflated.* EUSEBIUS *sees a chance to rub salt in the wound.*

Was that Mary I saw you talking to?

TARRY (*Refusing to be drawn*) Maybe it was.

> *Awkward silence.*

EUSEBIUS (*Goading*) You were lucky you wasn't offered one of them oul' jobs at the Mission —

TARRY (*Struggling to save face, but stung and unconvincing*) I sent word to Father Markey not to give me out.

EUSEBIUS You did. I'd say you did alright.

TARRY (*Changing subject, trying to recover something*) Still, if you got the name of being seen with one of the Duffys you'd be ruined.

EUSEBIUS (*Limply*) You would, I suppose.

> EUSEBIUS *ponders the danger of this.*

TARRY I heard the bailiffs were seen coming from Carlins'.

EUSEBIUS They have a pad betten (*path beaten*) up to them. They'll be sold out before long.

TARRY Indeed they will not, Eusebius; they're not that far gone.

> EUSEBIUS *and* TARRY *settle separately into the prospect of acquiring Carlins'. Both are scheming. Then* EUSEBIUS *reacts as if he's remembered a bit of business.*

EUSEBIUS I'll be moving on another step. There's a man

coming with a mare.

Exits.

TARRY looks around, dreaming he'd conjure Mary again. Slowly his attitude, his whole posture, changes. Gradually he enters a realm of quiet reflection.

TARRY Is it natural, this need, the hunger I have to be near these whitethorn ditches, the lush nettles and docks and tufts of grass? All that's food and drink to me — the rutted lane banked with wild carrot like girls in their communion dresses in the May procession, and the dandelions like little golden stars in a big green sky, and that full four acres of potatoes coming into blossom. Even if I work from stars to stars, living from hand to mouth, I'm — happy. You'd go to the fair and come back thinking the whin bushes ought to know you. I mind a day, a wet day in April, and we were sowing oats, and I felt the sharp wind blowing hope and sadness, and I could see myself as I was looking out across the hedge at the long shiny road stretching far away, beyond these hills.

Pause.

Why is it we're always doing things against our will? Why do we fight what we want? Someday maybe I'll grow wings and fly away. But for now, yes, I'm happy. I love every step of this (*quiet, hesitant*) blooming place.

Pause. He sees someone approaching, recovers, and starts to busy himself. MRS FLYNN enters.

MRS FLYNN (*Looking into the field*) How do you think they're doing?

TARRY (*Overdoing it, to compensate, conceal*) The best turnips in the country. They're a dread. Some of them as

35

	thick as your thumb already. They're fierce turnips altogether.
MRS FLYNN	Don't be always boasting like the Tallons. The Tallons never had anything that wasn't better than anyone else. You may thank me they're as good as they are. Only I was at you you wouldn't sow them that evening. Let the others do the praising. Nothing I hate as much as a man that's always boasting about his own things. There's that Mrs Tallon and nobody has anything but her, to hear her talking. Her three skinny cows give more milk and more butter than anyone else's. Her geese are swans. (*Her real purpose*) Was that Eusebius you had with you?
TARRY	(*Defensive*) Ah, he was just passing. I hardly had time to talk to him.

She gives him a look.

MRS FLYNN	Did ye see the smile of him? There's more in that thing's head than a comb could take out. Oh, that's the right careful boy that knows how to make a shilling. There was two mares up there this morning to his stallion — and you always making little of that animal, not sixteen hands high. It's a terror the trade he's getting for that young horse.
TARRY	He'll get all the bad pays the first year, don't you know that? A new stallion or a new bull is like a new shop. Nobody ever made money off a stallion or a bull.
MRS FLYNN	Oh, that'll do you now. An oul' rake, like your Uncle Petey (*ever ready to vent her spleen about Uncle Petey*), the same Uncle Petey who knew everything, nobody could talk to him, oh no, he knew it all — he wouldn't make a shilling out of a stallion — and the whole country in stitches behind his back — no, he wouldn't, nor oul' Patsy Meegan, that crooked oul' bachelor — but I'll bet you Eusebius won't be so. They'll all pay Eusebius, that's for sure.

Nothing surer.

She moves her gaze away over towards Carlins'.

Them Carlins are unfortunate people. The whole farm — and that's the good dry farm — all going wild. Yellow weeds like a forest. Oh, that was a bad family that couldn't have luck. When a party quits going to Mass it's a poor sign. The abuse they used to give their father and mother was a total dread. Getting up in the morning, and if the tay wasn't fresh more would have to be wet. And there was a time when Jemmy was as consaitey (*conceited*) a boy as stepped into Dargan chapel. And all the girls that were after him! 'I could thatch a house with all the women I could get,' says he to me. 'Yes, I could thatch a house with all of them.'

Pause. She returns to her first point of interest.

Had Eusebius any news?

TARRY Curse o' god o' the ha'porth.

MRS FLYNN Catch that fellow to tell you anything! They tell me the grippers were up at Carlins' again. They'll be out of that before you're much older. They'll be on the broad road as sure as sure. And mind you, that's as dry and warm a farm of land as there is in the whole parish. There's a couple of fields there, and do you know what it is, you could plough them with a pair of donkeys, they're that free.

TARRY (*Recognizing her drift*) Do you know what I'm thinking?

MRS FLYNN What?

TARRY I'm thinking if you were clever you might slip in and get the place for half-nothing.

MRS FLYNN (*Rising, at his slowness*) And did it never occur to you that the same Eusebius Cassidy might be thinking that already, that his eyesight may be as good — or better? He'd see through a deal board, that one. (*More encouraging, wanting the best for her family after all*) It's a terrible pity you wouldn't take a better interest in your work and you could be the independentest man. Oh yes, the independentest man, and then you could tell all the beggars in Ireland to go and kiss your arse!

End of Act One.

ACT TWO

Scene One

Kitchen. Later that evening. MRS FLYNN, AGGIE, BRIDIE. TARRY *comes in, in good clothes, from the Mission.*

MRS FLYNN (*To* TARRY) Take off that good suit and not have everything on the one rack like the Carlins. Give Bridie a hand to teem that pot.

AGGIE They came all the way from Dundalk, you know.

> MRS FLYNN *looks puzzled, wonders what she's talking about?*

MRS FLYNN The Carlins?

BRIDIE No, the priests. For the Mission.

AGGIE And one was telling about a girl that met a boy and (*emphasized*) as a result (*knowing looks*) the girl committed suicide.

BRIDIE She was found in a well.

AGGIE And the preacher said, said he, (*every word emphasized*) 'That man damned that girl's soul'. That's what he said.

BRIDIE His very words.

> TARRY *shuffles, fidgets uneasily.*

MRS FLYNN (*Suddenly, savagely*) Wasn't there two of them in it!

> *All accept the wisdom of this. Pause.*

(*To* TARRY) You were a long time in the box with the priest, I hear. Did you kill a man or what? (*Notices*

BRIDIE *and* AGGIE *are interested*) What did you say that made him keep you so long?

TARRY (*Stalling*) It's a sin to tell a thing like that.

MRS FLYNN Whatever you do anyway, I wouldn't like to think of you knocking around Duffys' house, not that I'd ever believe you'd do anything, but you know the big-mouths that's about this place.

TARRY You needn't worry.

BRIDIE (*Not letting the opportunity slip away*) Don't you know well what they're saying about him and the priest?

MRS FLYNN What? Now what?

AGGIE (*As Fr Markey*) Now, my son, what sins do you remember since your last Confessions?

BRIDIE (*As Tarry, exaggerated: again the family — except* TARRY *this time — join in the pleasure of these mimicries*) I read books, Father.

AGGIE (*As Fr Markey*) Books? What sort of books?

BRIDIE (*As Tarry, mumbling, unsure*) Eh, Shaw, Father.

AGGIE (*As Fr Markey*) Shaw? You should be reading *The Messenger of the Sacred Heart*. Do you ever read the little *Messenger*?

BRIDIE (*As Tarry*) Yes, Father.

AGGIE (*As Fr Markey*) Continue to read it, my child; in that little book you'll find all you need. And give up this man Shaw.

MRS FLYNN (*Throwing her eyes to heaven*) We'll be the talk of the country.

> *This ends the play.* BRIDIE, *after a moment, goes upstairs.* AGGIE *looks after her, and follows.*

(*To* TARRY) Did you hear that one of the Missioners was up with the Carlins trying to get them to come out to the Mission.

TARRY They're not going?

MRS FLYNN Going, how are you? Aye. And you're taking pattern by them. (*Thinking to herself a moment*) Do you know what? I think I'll dodge up one of these evenings. I don't know the day or hour I was last in Carlins'.

Since the Mission I hear they don't get up till evening.

TARRY and MRS FLYNN *conspiratorial in the possibilities in her plan. Then, returning to the practicalities.*

You brought the heifer to be covered? Had you much trouble with her?

TARRY (*Looking for sympathy*) Plenty.

No response.

But I managed.

MRS FLYNN We'd better put her in for the night and not have the other cows lepping on her. I hope she keeps.

Pause. Confidentially, to TARRY.

Patsy Meegan sent word the day.

TARRY About what?

MRS FLYNN He has a notion of Bridie. But don't breathe a word of this to a soul.

TARRY (*Astonished, amused*) Patsy Meegan!

MRS FLYNN The Missioners must have shook him up.

TARRY He's a bit past himself, wouldn't you say? Weren't you saying yourself, the crooked oul' bachelor —

MRS FLYNN Arra, nonsense. He's a good, sober, industrious boy — with a damn good farm of land in Miskin. And an empty house. Girls can't be too stiff these days. They're all hard pleased and easy fitted.

TARRY But he must be well over the sixty mark! That man's sixty if he's a day.

MRS FLYNN (*Her view so changed, now that there's a chance he'll take* BRIDIE *off her hands*) That's young enough for a healthy man. And, mind you, Bridie is no spring chicken. Only the day I was thinking she's within a kick of thirty. If she gets him she'll be lucky. Whatever about the Aggie one, herself and the process-server, and the devil the big rush is on him.

As Charlie Trainor says about them daughters, they're like horse dung, you never walk the road but you meet them. I always say, marry the first man that asks you. Yes, I was thinking, I might dander up by Carlins' to have a look-see.

> *She readies herself and goes out purposefully. Pause. Suddenly* TARRY *is attentive to heavy footsteps approaching the door. Visitor's cough to announce arrival.* PATSY MEEGAN *comes in, an oldish man trying to be young in his talk and actions. He tries to straighten his humped shoulders, and to sprightly his step.*
>
> *Extreme awkwardness.* TARRY *looking in all directions for help, trying to make* PATSY *welcome and, at the same time, wishing he were elsewhere.*

TARRY Patsy. It's yourself. How's things?

PATSY The best. Never better. Fierce great weather.

TARRY It is surely.

PATSY How's all the care?

TARRY Damn the bother.

PATSY That's the way. There's a grand stretch in the evenings now.

TARRY (*As if this is a revelation*) There is, is right. Come in, come in.

> PATSY *looks around, obviously disappointed that* TARRY *is alone.*

So how's things, Patsy?

PATSY Not so bad. I was just passing —

> *Neither he nor* TARRY *believes this.* PATSY *looks around again, resigns himself to* TARRY's *company. The conversation is strained. In another place or setting, the same talk might be natural.*

A sup of rain would do no harm.

TARRY   Who wants rain?

PATSY   Sure the cattle are starved for a mouthful of grass. You didn't sell your heifer.

TARRY   I'll hold her a while.

PATSY   It's often said you were better sorry for selling than sorry for not selling. (*Recovering: he doesn't want to offend*) Nice wee stuff, though. (*But he can't stop himself*) A bit rough o' the head all the same.

TARRY   She'll have to be doing.

PATSY   (*Philosophically*) She has the makings of a good bag, a bit shy in the back left quarter, but the makings of a good bag all the same. (PATSY's *discomfort and unhappiness prompts the mean word*) Still a cow could drop dead in the morning, and think of the loss then. It's not the day a baste (*beast*) dies that ye miss it.

TARRY   You've fair good ones yourself?

PATSY   Not so bleddy bad, as the fella said.

TARRY   Do you think will there be a price for them?

PATSY   God knows. Though there should be — (*Determined to praise*) Your turnips is doing terrible well.

TARRY   They're a holy living dread. No natural crow could pull one of them turnips.

> *They have exhausted the topics that come to mind. Long silence.*

PATSY   Well, that's the way.

TARRY   That's the way.

> PATSY *produces a packet of cigarettes, opens it, and offers one.*

PATSY   You wouldn't have a match on you?

TARRY   You're getting swanky.

PATSY   Well, that's the way. (PATSY *plays variations on this phrase to break the silences*)

TARRY   (*Unable to stop himself*) That's the way.

> TARRY *gets up to put on the kettle.*

Where the devil's these women of ours?

> PATSY *is all ears but doesn't answer. He gets up to rub the arch of the fire.*

PATSY The man that built that arch knew his job.
TARRY (*Relief at a subject*) The Ring Finnegan.
PATSY He was the right smoke doctor. (*Without much enthusiasm*) The Ring Finnegan.

> TARRY *goes to the door to listen and look up and down. Obviously no one is coming.*

I suppose I'm as well be on the move.
TARRY (*Not meaning it*) Aw, take your time.
PATSY As the man said, I have a few things to do and, like that, I'd better go before night falls.
TARRY That kettle's near boiling.
PATSY (*Facing the reality*) No, I'm better be going. (*At the doorway, trying to be casual*) I suppose — I suppose these women of yours won't be home for a while.
TARRY The mother ought to be home anyway, and you're as well wait.
PATSY I'll not. Sure I can come some other evening.

> PATSY *departs.* TARRY *collapses with relief, though he's vexed that he had to deal with the visit himself. Almost immediately,* MRS FLYNN *returns.*

MRS FLYNN What have you the kettle on for?
TARRY Sure who do you think was here?
MRS FLYNN Who?
TARRY (*As Patsy*) That's-the-way.
MRS FLYNN What are you saying?
TARRY Patsy-that's-the-way. Patsy Meegan.
MRS FLYNN And where is he now? (*Seeing a lost chance*) And where was that one?
TARRY Where was anyone? He's gone.
MRS FLYNN And when will he be back? Did he say he'd be

back?

TARRY (*Punishing her*) He said he might and he mightn't.

MRS FLYNN The devil thrapple her anyway. Where did she go? Why is it she's never here when she's wanted?

TARRY She's above. Listening and laughing at every that's-the-way.

Pause.

MRS FLYNN You may as well make a sup now when you have the kettle boiled. If I had to be here I'd tell her something. Yes, hard pleased and easy fitted, that's what she is. Oh, I saw ones like her before and they'd want a man made for them. Ah-ha, I saw them after, and they weren't so stiff.

TARRY All the same she'll hardly take him.

MRS FLYNN She will, you know, she will surely. She's not going to lie up on me here and a man coming looking for her. She'll marry him or take the broad road. She'll learn alright what way's the way. You made this tea too strong. We'll not be able to sleep after this. And if that Bridie one goes, the other might too.

TARRY (*Warming to it*) That's a fact. They say she's horrid great with Tommy Quinn.

MRS FLYNN *is determined not to let him bask in the prospect of the house to himself. She puts her concerns aside and returns to her cause.*

MRS FLYNN Do you know what, I'm just after coming down from Carlins' and there's not a thing about the place that Eusebius hasn't whipped over to his own — the roller that you were always saying you could get and the good reaping mill.

TARRY There was a good Ransome mowing-machine I could be doing with —

MRS FLYNN And never in saecula will those articles be returned. Still, I have a little plan of me own and if all goes well we might do better than so.

TARRY   Will they ever be able to pay the debts?

MRS FLYNN   Never. Oh, never. Sure they're there and there's not the slightest bit of worry on them, no more than if they were made of money. I was putting it on to her about selling the cow — she's as good a cow on her third calf as there is in the country — and I might as well be talking to the wall. They laughed at me. Laughed.

She goes to the bottom of the stairs and listens.

Do you hear those two? They'll be heard where they won't be seen. (*Calls*) Come on down, the pair of you.

No answer.

Bridie! Aggie! (*Resolute*) Right. We'll start without them.

She and TARRY *kneel. The Rosary begins.* TARRY *sighs with the weight of the world, but is gradually embraced by the music of the prayer.*

MRS FLYNN   Hail Mary, full of grace, the Lord is with thee. Blessèd art thou amongst women, and blessèd is the fruit of thy womb, Jesus.

TARRY   Holy Mary (*pauses at name — and goes on with feeling*), Mother of God, pray for us sinners, now and at the hour of our death. Amen.

Scene Two

Kitchen. A few days later. MRS FLYNN *at chores, with* BRIDIE *and* AGGIE. MRS FLYNN *goes to the window as she frequently does, and then to the door.*

MRS FLYNN   Bedad, there's someone coming in from the Big Road. It's — Come here you (BRIDIE) that has the good sight.

BRIDIE   It's — is it Tommy Quinn? The process-server?

They look at AGGIE, *who starts to straighten her hair.*

Aggie, you that's got your eye on him, go out and bring him in till we hear what he has to say.

AGGIE   (*Flustered*) Where's the clean apron?

Her mother hands it to her. AGGIE *exits.*

MRS FLYNN   How long is she going with him?

BRIDIE   Since after the Mission.

MRS FLYNN   Does he mean business?

BRIDIE   How?

MRS FLYNN   Is he the marrying kind?

BRIDIE   It'd be hard to say rightly.

AGGIE returns with TOMMY, *a friendly fellow, on terms of goodwill with everyone, and never averse to letting anyone read through his bunch of civil bills and summonses.*

MRS FLYNN   Ah, Tommy, it's yourself. You'll have a cup?

TOMMY   No, no. I wouldn't have time.

The others look: he has all the time in the world. TOMMY *looks at the clock.*

Places to go. Things to do.

MRS FLYNN The busy man. Give no heed to that oul' clock. It never told the truth in its life. (*The others look at each other in surprise*) But what has you up our way?

TOMMY The usual fare, Mrs Flynn. Important business.

MRS FLYNN Oh I know, I know.

TOMMY (*Yielding, flicks through a sheaf of pink documents*) There's one for Joe Connolly of Lisdrum, and here's another for Jack Hamill —

MRS FLYNN'*s quiet satisfaction in this news;* AGGIE'*s and* BRIDIE'*s curiosity, trying to read ahead, over his shoulder etc.*

MRS FLYNN Musha, what's the matter with Joe Connolly?

BRIDIE Sure he's one of the best-off men in the county.

AGGIE (*As if this proved something*) I saw him in the market last Wednesday week.

TOMMY I had one here somewhere — (*The others tantalized; almost aside*) Joe is in trouble over a girl. The father is suing him for — seduction!

MRS FLYNN Ah, you're a liar, Tommy. That man's seventy if he's a day —

BRIDIE And a grown family.

AGGIE (*Again, as if this made a difference*) Of boys and girls of his own.

MRS FLYNN I wouldn't even it to him.

TOMMY There you are —

BRIDIE⎫
AGGIE ⎭ (*As Patsy, their private joke*) That's the way.

TOMMY It's hard to be up to the men that's going these days. (*Concentrating*) I had one here and whatever the hell happened to it. Aha, there she is. Have a look at that one.

Eager, all eyes.

MRS FLYNN For Father Markey!

BRIDIE That's a terror!

AGGIE That bates (*beats*) all.

BRIDIE (*Studying it carefully*) Fifty pound in debt! Doesn't *he* live high?

AGGIE The parish priest! Who'd think that?

TOMMY He'll hardly let it go to Court.

MRS FLYNN (*Storing the information in her mind*) But sure we all know now. (*Pause*) I suppose you're going up to Carlins'.

TOMMY I have three bills for them today — one for Tom and two for Jemmy — and, sure, like that, I have orders to seize for the past years. I don't like to lift the cow. That Eusebius is grazing the ground but you'd never catch a beast of his about, though I could have taken a pair of bullocks once. And would you believe me, Mrs Flynn, (*his one moment of unkindness*) he never as much as said thank you. No, a mean man.

AGGIE Mean is no name for Eusebius Cassidy, Tommy.

BRIDIE Sure we live beside him.

TARRY *comes in, overhears the end of this and, while he might know it to be true, is offended.*

MRS FLYNN Would you say would any greedy devil buy the place on the quiet, Tommy?

TOMMY It's possible. I heard that a couple of offers were made. But I couldn't be sure.

MRS FLYNN Wouldn't they ate you for land around here?

TOMMY Ate is right. But I'd best be off. (*Greeting*) Well, Tarry. You're winning?

TARRY (*Confused, caught off guard*) Aw now —

AGGIE I'll be down the road a bit with you, Tommy.

TOMMY, *delighted with himself, exits with* AGGIE.

MRS FLYNN (*To* TARRY) Well, what do you think of that?

TARRY (*Stalling*) It'd be hard to say —

MRS FLYNN You're the slackest man I ever met! Some fine day some cute boy will slip in and buy the place over all our heads. Mark my words. And we'll be left and laughed at, like your Uncle Petey.

A brainwave. Suddenly busies herself. She starts to get ready for the town. TARRY *notices her all dressed up, somewhat ridiculous.*

TARRY Where are you going?
MRS FLYNN I've a mind to go as far as the town. That farm's been 'up on the wall' for years and no one in a hurry to make the first offer.
TARRY You'll hardly make a bid in the face of Joe Finnegan? Sure his land borders the Carlins'. His brother Larry's well known for being a hard man. (*That is, in a brawl*)
MRS FLYNN I know they say they're relations but the same Larry was charged with stealing, and that changes the lie of the land.
TARRY That could open the gate, alright.

She's ready but can't stop fussing.

MRS FLYNN Don't forget when I'm in the town to clean that drink for the cattle in the Low Field.
TARRY Don't you know well I won't.
MRS FLYNN And you might clean out them hen houses and whitewash the roosts.

TARRY *knows all this.*

TARRY Go on, go on, go on if you're going.
MRS FLYNN The roosts need to be whitewashed once a week in the summer. (*Pause*) I'd better be going.
TARRY Go on. Go on before you change your mind.

She goes to the door.

MRS FLYNN You might wish me luck.

Suddenly it's obvious that she's terrified.

TARRY Of course I wish you luck. But just to satisfy you, Good luck and all the luck in the world.

MRS FLYNN (*As if blessed by this*) Thank you, and mind yourself till I come back. (*She can't quite let go*) And keep that gate shut, Tarry. I see that hungry sow of Tallons' prowling down there at the turn.

She goes out. TARRY is left with BRIDIE.

TARRY (*Out of the blue, he pronounces like a priest, as if he's addressing a congregation and not an individual*) All this foreign dancing and music is poison. It never belonged in this country.

BRIDIE gives him a look, then lights a cigarette with a live coal.

BRIDIE What the bleddy hell are you trying to say?

TARRY You know damn well what I mean.

BRIDIE Ah dry up and don't be making a barney-balls of yourself. I'm starved for a smoke.

TARRY (*Growling*) You're gone to hell alright.

BRIDIE Amn't I as much entitled to smoke as you. I'm smoking dry tea-leaves this last month and the mouth is burned off me. (*She's winning*) Come on, we'll have tea. I'm as well have a bit of gas while I can.

TARRY Supposing Patsy Meegan saw you, wouldn't that be a fine how-are-you?

BRIDIE Do you know what, fellas like you that never as much as had their arm around a girl always think that there's nothing in a bit of a coort only the one thing. That's all that's in your heads.

TARRY But what about Patsy? Are you ever going to marry him?

BRIDIE Do I look out of my mind?

TARRY Ah, but you shouldn't be making a fool of yourself, having the neighbours talking.

BRIDIE What do I care what they're saying? (*Still, she's*

anxious to know) What were they saying anyway?

TARRY   I only heard that one of the McArdles was up here with Patsy and singing his praises the other night.

BRIDIE *tries to dismiss the thought.*

TARRY   Oh yes, he was saying —

He sing-songs the voice and sayings of McArdle, as if memorized, and warms to the recitation the further he goes on. BRIDIE *joins in with their mother's answers, knowing well what they'd be.*

TARRY   (*As McArdle*) Here (*making a big gesture of pointing at where Patsy might be*), here is none of your fly-the-kites. He could go where there's more money but he's not looking for money. No, he's not looking for money. Good men aren't got on the tops of bushes these days. He has fourteen acres of what-you-might-call good land with a way to water in every field. He doesn't owe a penny piece to any man. He only lives across the hill and if ever you wanted a turn done you wouldn't be stuck.

BRIDIE   (*As Mrs Flynn, conceding*) He's as good a take as any young girl could want in these bad times.

TARRY   (*As McArdle*) Or, you may say, in *any* times.

BRIDIE   (*Not sure about this; then, as Mrs Flynn*) Whatever you say. But what's the use of talking? Can I make her marry the man?

TARRY   (*As McArdle*) Mind, I'm not saying she's ould, but it's time she was getting a man. (BRIDIE *stirs uncomfortably*) I don't want to make little of any woman's daughter, but amn't I only saying what's right? What are you going to do about it?

BRIDIE   (*As Mrs Flynn, rallying*) What *can* I do about it?

TARRY   (*As McArdle*) Surely you can drive in the heifer?

BRIDIE   (*As Mrs Flynn*) Like oul' hell I can. (*Then, as herself again*) And I know well Patsy sat there all the while, as pleased and proud as punch, and as tight shut as a crow's arse.

TARRY   There's something, something unnatural about that man.

Perhaps for the first time BRIDIE *feels a trace of sympathy in her brother.*

BRIDIE   Anyway, it's all codology. The dirty oul' crooked eejit. It's saying his prayers he ought to be. (TARRY *laughs*) Oul' eejit, oul' eejit. (*As if trying to convince herself. Then, to change the subject*) Here, are you looking for a fag? I have a couple here. I'll give you one.

TARRY   (*Instantly defensive*) No, I don't want a fag. (*Searching*) Haven't I one of my own — somewhere.

She reaches one to him. He takes it, but doesn't thank her.

(*To break the silence*) Still, you'll hardly marry him —

Pause. He registers her lack of agreement.

Surely to God you wouldn't marry a thing like that! How could you bring yourself to go to bed — (*surprise*) — with a hairy oul' thing like Patsy?

BRIDIE   That could be got over.

TARRY   (*Alarmed by the true possibility*) You're not that hard up for a man!

BRIDIE   Am I not?

The dreadful thought silences them both and surrounds them in pity. Then, after a long pause, to concede some tenderness in the misery

That Mary Reilly's mad for you.

TARRY *starts.*

Didn't I hear her?

> TARRY *is flustered. This is* BRIDIE's *awkward way to persuade him not to forgo love.*

Go on. Make a rush at it same as if you were taking a dose of salts. Sure she'll hardly take a bite out of you.

TARRY Ah, quit.

BRIDIE You just want to be pushed. You're like all the others. Shy but willing, like a bride in bed.

TARRY (*Unable to face this*) Ah, don't bother me, don't bother me. Such talk! I never want to hear another word about her.

> *Emotional emptiness and chaos.*
> *Quick curtain.*

Scene Three

Eight o'clock, Thursday evening. Brighter light as suggested earlier.
TARRY *is waiting at the lane. His hair combed, etc. He fidgets, paces,
is obviously nervous. He looks each and every way. Even his good
clothes have a patch, stains, etc.*

TARRY Better an hour early than a minute late. (*Then, after
thinking about this*) Ach — I'll count to fifty and then
she'll have come. (*He mouths the numbers, voice up
in the 40s, and much slower*) Forty-six, forty-seven,
forty-eight, forty-nine — (*Suddenly*) I knew it. I knew
it. Knew it all along.

Suddenly MARY *is there, an apparition.*

MARY (*Quietly*) Hello.
TARRY Hello. (*Their awkward pauses begin again*) I wasn't
expecting you —
MARY Didn't I say I'd come?
TARRY I was just thinking of going when you came.
MARY You were not.
TARRY That's a clouting evening for the spuds.
MARY Do you think so, Tarry? (*Whatever he says is wonder-
ful*) Sit down here, sit down on the tail of this coat.

They manage this. TARRY's *hand is near hers on the
bank. He tries to move it towards her but it will not
go.*

TARRY Yes. Yes. It's a clouting evening alright. For the
spuds, I mean.
MARY You must come up to the house some evening, Tarry.
TARRY Oh God, no. Not at all. (*He chides himself*) Sure Father
Markey and everybody does be up there.
MARY What harm?
TARRY (*Coming to think of it*) I don't know. They say he does
be near living in your place these days. Nothing for

55

the priests only the rich. My mother said that he's going to get you into some music school in Dublin. She says you're a great player of the piano —

MARY (*Shyly*) I am not.

TARRY And Father Markey's very interested in the music. She asked if I was ever speaking to you. An odd time, says I. Do you know, she's not nearly as fine a girl as she was a couple of years ago. (TARRY, *scrabbling to find something/anything to say, says all the wrong things. But it doesn't matter*)

MARY Were you ever talking to him?

TARRY (*Bravado, and a lie*) I never was talking to a priest in my life.

MARY (*To flatter him*) I'd say he'd think you're great.

TARRY (*And this is as bold as it gets*) What would a priest say if he saw us now?

MARY Aye, just.

Pause.

He has a brother who writes plays.

TARRY Who? Father Markey?

MARY *nods.*

TARRY By the holies!

MARY *shuts her eyes softly, and leans her head towards* TARRY *who, instead of yielding/accepting her invitation, stiffens. She straightens up. Her disappointment is growing.*

TARRY We'd better be getting back.

But they remain, in confused rapture. TARRY *simply does not know what to say or how to act.*

MARY Will you be at the dance on Sunday night, after the concert?

TARRY Dancing's an eejit's game. What would you say to a bunch of horses that after a hard day's work spent the night galloping and careering round the field? I wouldn't dream of wasting any time at a dance.

MARY (*Ignoring him, knowing it's not what he wants to say*) I'll be there. (*Sweetly*) And I'd love you to come.

TARRY I wouldn't bother me bleddy head.

MARY Still, you're apt to be there —

TARRY An eejit's game.

MARY Sunday night will be a big event, Tarry. (*Reasoning, and spelling it out*) I could see you there.

TARRY Indeed you couldn't and don't be pretending you could. (*The real reason*) That's all for big people (*people with money*).

MARY (*Her disappointment becoming desperation and annoyance, but persisting*) You'll probably be there all the same —

TARRY I wouldn't be seen dead in that hall. This dancing is all a cod. I never knew a dancer who was worth his grub to a farmer.

He realizes what he is saying and starts to berate himself. As he turns to apologize, somehow her heart breaks into

MARY The trouble with you, Tarry Flynn, is — you don't know what you want!

She rushes off in tears.

TARRY Oh my God. What's the matter with me? Why couldn't I say the right things? Why couldn't I say what I meant? (*Pathetic*) The gentle things I'm well able to say in my head at work out in the fields?

Then pulling himself together, and looking down at his boots and — worse — his trousers.

Those bloody trousers! I declare it's all their fault.

Scene Four

Kitchen, later that night. Near dark. AGGIE *and* BRIDIE, *with* TARRY *in the same clothes, miserable.* MRS FLYNN *comes in, back from the town.*

AGGIE   Well?

BRIDIE   Well? You're very late.

MRS FLYNN *plops in a seat.*

MRS FLYNN   Bridie, will you throw a handful of oats to them hens and not have them picking at the window as if they never got a bite. Tarry, did you see about the cattle?

The suspense is prolonged.

TARRY   Didn't I say I would.

MRS FLYNN   And whitewash the roosts?

TARRY   Yes, yes. How did it go?

MRS FLYNN *ignores the question.*

MRS FLYNN   From now on you'll have to change your gait of going.

She studies him.

Is that a rip in your good clothes? Lord, but I can't let you out of my sight but you're liable to do yourself harm, break your neck or something. Bridie, pull over the kettle and don't wet the tay till I get me breath.

TARRY   (*Impatient*) But how did you get on?

MRS FLYNN   (*With the full import of what she's managed*) I'm making you independent of the beggars, Tarry.

TARRY   You got it then, you got it! How much?

MRS FLYNN How much do you think?

TARRY How would I know?

MRS FLYNN Well, make a guess.

TARRY (*Thinking this a wild, high guess*) A hundred — a hundred and twenty.

MRS FLYNN (*Disappointed*) Ah, you're the man that should be sent to buy a thing. (*To* BRIDIE) Give me over me handbag from the table. (*To* TARRY) Yes, you're the man that ought to be sent.

She takes out a document and pushes it in front of him.

Have a look at that, you that's the scholar. (*Turning*) You make the tay, Aggie.

TARRY (*Amazed*) Two hundred and fifty! (*Straightening*) Of course it's worth twice that. I only mentioned the hundred and twenty because I thought maybe you got it cheap.

MRS FLYNN Do you know what that place is worth? Do you know how much the solicitor said he could get for that place if the Carlins were out?

The others don't dare venture a guess.

See! (*Pause. To* BRIDIE) I believe the Cassidy one is home.

BRIDIE Were you talking to her?

MRS FLYNN (*Snaps*) No, I wasn't. She'll get a man this time or lose a fall. (*Looking at* TARRY) And for all that she's not a bad girl. Back to England she wouldn't go if she got the chance of a man.

BRIDIE (*Sarcastically, looking at* TARRY) She came to the right place, so.

MRS FLYNN Eusebius offered a hundred. That's about all the money they have in spite of the stallion. From now on you'll have to put an inch to your step and quit your dreaming.

Pause. She drinks tea. Then she takes off her shoes,
stretches her feet.

Lord, these shoes had the feet burned off me.

Everyone ponders the new acquisition.

(*Musing aloud*) Not a bad girl at all. Far from it.
And I'm sure they'd give all they have if she got a
good catch. And mind you, Molly Brady — (TARRY
cringes) — is a good healthy girl that'd do a bad
turn to no man.

BRIDIE *and* AGGIE *recognize a familiar drift, and leave.*

(*To* TARRY) In two or three years it's you that could
be the independent man. These ones will be going
sooner or later.

She pauses to wonder how.

And remember, Tarry, it's not of meself I'm thinking. That little place of Bradys' would put a real
bone in yours. If you'd take a fool's advice you
could be richer than anyone here. Look at Eusebius
cutting calves and pigs and every damn thing to
make a penny; and Charlie Trainor that'd lift a
ha'penny out of the dung with his teeth. Oh, it's
well I know these parties and that's why I'd like
you to be independent of the whole rick-ma-tick of
them. I wouldn't be bothered with these ones that
you do be talking about — that Reilly one (TARRY *is*
stung), that poor girl, everyone belonging to her
died of consumption. And the trouble she was in
up at the Cross. Who's to say some of it wasn't her
own fault. That Molly Brady's no fallen goods.

TARRY (*Disarmed a moment, relaxes to admit*) A man married
to Molly Brady could be comfortable, that's a fact.

MRS FLYNN There's seven of as nice a field up there as there is

in the parish. If you gave them any kind of mind-
ing it's you that could take out the crop.

TARRY (*Without it being clear whether he approves*) It would
be an easy way.

> MRS FLYNN *relaxes into her dreams for the place and
> for* TARRY *who is clearly less than happy with her hopes.*

MRS FLYNN Whatever you do don't go up next or near the
Carlins' for the present. You'd get a false kick or a
prod of a graip, and that's what 'ud please Eusebius.
They'd all love to see a big row now. Big Lip Larry
Finnegan over there is making out to be a friend of
theirs; he's not a full fourth cousin. I'm nearly as
close meself. Damn them anyway. (*Trailing off*) The
best of a farm if it was minded.

Scene Five

Outside. A few days later. EUSEBIUS *and* HUGHIE *in silent conversation, excited.* CHARLIE *comes by.*

EUSEBIUS Well? Did you hear?

CHARLIE Hear what?

EUSEBIUS About the row.

CHARLIE The row? What row? I only heard Joe Finnegan was lepping mad at the Flynns' buying of the place over his head. Threatening to make it hot for them.

EUSEBIUS There'll be sport about this, there'll be sport alright.

CHARLIE Sport about what? Tell me what's after happening?

> *Throughout what follows* CHARLIE *is an interested and delighted spectator.*

EUSEBIUS There was a row the day between Tarry and Joe, an unholy row down by the march between their places when Tarry was fencing. (*As Joe Finnegan*) I'll break his bloody neck, says Joe. And Joe's wife beside him and says she, (*as Mrs Finnegan*) Joe, Joe, be careful, for you know as well as bread that that man isn't like another. Look out for yourself for he's not square.

> *They all nod at the idea.*

(*As Joe*) I'm make him square, Maggie. Give me the graip, give me the graip. By the sweet and living God he's not going to cut my bushes.

HUGHIE (*Interrupting, and continuing, as Joe*) Tarry Flynn, I'll get you, I'll get you, says he. You hure you, you hure, Flynn (*we get the impression as he looks to* EUSEBIUS *for verification that* EUSEBIUS *must actually have witnessed this*), you're a hure like every one belonging to you. The good big bush!

EUSEBIUS (*Softly, seriously, as Tarry*) If you come out here, says

62

Tarry, I may as well tell you, (*quicker*) I'll cut the
head off you. I'll cut it off. (*Slower*) Do you hear
that?

HUGHIE So it's through the gap in the ditch like a bullet
with Joe and the two of them then face to face.

> HUGHIE *and* EUSEBIUS *square to each other,* EUSEBIUS
> *with comic exaggeration of* TARRY *posed à la Queens-*
> *berry rules. They act out the exchange.* HUGHIE *(as*
> *Joe) brawling,* EUSEBIUS *(as Tarry) poised. Then 'Tarry'*
> *lands a perfect punch on 'Joe'. Suddenly* TARRY *comes*
> *in on their re-enactment. Recognizes immediately*
> *what's been going on.*

EUSEBIUS (*Trying to recover, for everyone*) There you are! The
hard man! The hard man!

CHARLIE (*Sees* TARRY's *billhook*) You're fencing?

TARRY (*Begins to answer*) Sticking a few bushes in gaps —

> *They all attempt, and fail, to suppress laughter at the*
> *thought.*

EUSEBIUS A good bleddy idea — (*but it's useless, the subject's*
too close to the other, and all, except TARRY, *find it hard*
not to burst out laughing. EUSEBIUS *tries to change the*
subject, to the old reliable) See any women lately?

TARRY (*Falling for it*) I was talking to May Tallon last night
— (*He sees an opportunity to score a point on one of the*
conspirators)

EUSEBIUS You were? Had she any stir?

TARRY If you but knew. (*Looking at* CHARLIE, *who shuffles*
uncomfortably)

HUGHIE Jaybers! What was she saying?

TARRY She was telling me someone followed her from the
Cross the other evening and tried his best to get
her to come out to Kerleys' hayfield with him.
(*Pointed, a world of resentment rearing*) What do you
think of that, Charlie?

They all look at CHARLIE. TARRY *has scored a point. The mood is unbearably strained.* CHARLIE *and* HUGHIE *look at each other and make to move.*

CHARLIE (*Limply*) Don't mind him. We'll dander another bit. (*To* EUSEBIUS) Are you coming?

EUSEBIUS I'll hang on a while.

> CHARLIE *and* HUGHIE *depart.* TARRY *is left with* EUSEBIUS *who, as usual, is trying to be on everyone's side.*

Right pack of savages, them Finnegans, wouldn't you say?

TARRY (*Trying to give nothing away, and with an edge anyway*) They're as good as anybody else, Eusebius. Do you ever be up there at all?

EUSEBIUS Do you know what, Tarry, I was up with them this morning. (TARRY *senses* EUSEBIUS *might have witnessed the row*) Joe borrowed me rope-twister last year and it was as much as I could do to get him to give it back when I went for it.

> TARRY'*s sceptical look makes an uneasy pause.*

I saw Joe's missus coming along the lane. (*He plays this out bit by bit, regaining the upper hand*) Going somewhere. Dressed.

TARRY (*As if to make little of it*) She could be going anywhere.

EUSEBIUS (*The final straw*) She had her hat on. So it must be something. Something serious, wouldn't you say?

> TARRY'*s heart sinks: she's going for the police or the doctor or both.*

TARRY (*Things are so bad they can hardly get worse*) Did you hear anything else on your travels?

EUSEBIUS Like what?

TARRY   Ah, nothing.

EUSEBIUS   Have you something yourself? (*Grasping the mystery, he looks closely at* TARRY) I have a kind of a notion you heard something. Don't be so bleddy close, Tarry. Go and tell a fella. You heard something?

TARRY   Don't you know very well I'd tell you if I heard anything? Don't you know that?

EUSEBIUS   (*Nodding doubtfully*) You might, I suppose.

TARRY   Well, it's hardly worth me while telling you. I was only thinking you might have heard something about the Brady one. She wasn't seen at Mass this past month, and people are talking, do you see?

EUSEBIUS   What do you mane — ?

TARRY   And the funny thing is, some people were trying to say that I was seen with her. Wouldn't that make you laugh, heh? Of course it's all Charlie's doing — wouldn't you say?

EUSEBIUS   That's a dread, a holy dread. That bates the little dish, as the fellow said. And are you going to do anything about it?

TARRY   Sure the thing isn't worth a word about it. Sure, Holy God —

EUSEBIUS   Well, are you?

TARRY   (*Struggling to convince*) There's no doubt about it, I can't help laughing when I think of it. Wouldn't it make a cat laugh, now wouldn't it?

EUSEBIUS   (*Seriously*) They say the woman's word is law.

TARRY   (*Resolute*) I'll fight it to the last ditch. I'll fight it.

EUSEBIUS   What else would you do? You'd need to get a first-class man.

TARRY   One of the young fellas, Eusebius, they wouldn't be so dear.

EUSEBIUS   I could tell you your best plan (*fishing for more information*), only I don't know enough about the case, Tarry. There's no point in dreaming up lies, you know.

TARRY   She can go to hell backwards. They'll get nothing off me. You can't take feathers off a frog, can ye?

EUSEBIUS   (*Direct*) You have Carlins'.

TARRY (*Wondering exactly how much he knows/what he means*) Maybe I have.

> EUSEBIUS *realizes he'll hear no more, for the moment — he suddenly looks busy as if he wants away to the next instalment.*

EUSEBIUS (*Limply*) I've just remembered. I've to go back for something I forgot.

> *Exits.* TARRY *alone with his worries.*
>
> PATSY MEEGAN *comes on with his short cough that interrupts* TARRY'*s deliberations. It's plain that* PATSY — *in a slightly 'distant' greeting — a nod — knows of the row. He studies* TARRY *carefully.*

TARRY (*As if accused by his look*) Well, he's a very thick man.

PATSY (*Considers*) He's a hasty man, but I wouldn't say he's a thick man.

TARRY I didn't hurt him very badly anyway. (*More friendly, seeking a friend*) Are you coming over this evening, Patsy?

PATSY (*With obvious less interest*) I might and I mightn't.

TARRY (*Suddenly, almost surprising himself in the desperation of it*) Dammit you're getting younger, Patsy, by the day.

PATSY (*Limply*) Keeping the best side out.

TARRY Anyway, you'll be welcome, Patsy, you'll be right welcome, you know that.

PATSY Indeed I do. Indeed I do.

TARRY (*Enticing, nearly pleading*) We'll all be waiting.

PATSY That's the way.

> *He strolls off confidently: the most eligible bachelor in the land.* TARRY *sinks into his own loneliness. Stands bleakly a long while.*
>
> *End of Act Two.*

ACT THREE

Scene One

Kitchen. Later that day. MRS FLYNN *busy.* TARRY *comes in slowly, the weight of the world on his shoulders, and now this.*

MRS FLYNN What in the name of God way did you come home? I sent Aggie up to see how you were getting on and she came back to tell me that hilt or hair of you wasn't to be seen, and that the devil damn the fence you did.

TARRY (*Appealing*) But wait till you hear.

MRS FLYNN Sure, God and His Blessèd Mother knows that I'm waiting —

TARRY (*Suddenly outspoken*) I suppose she didn't tell you that I was attacked by Joe Finnegan and very nearly killed. She didn't tell you that, no, but she told you that I didn't bush the gaps.

MRS FLYNN Arra, what's this you're saying?

TARRY Only the way I tackled him it might be a different story.

MRS FLYNN (*Beginning to consider that this might be a serious matter*) The Lord look down on us anyway — And may the devil thrapple that big-mouthed Joe that — that it's no wonder he hasn't a man child about the place. What did he say anyway?

TARRY It's not what he said, it's what he did — or tried to do. Came down the length of the ditch rushing at me like a bull, with a graip in his hand —

MRS FLYNN (*It is serious*) Lord bless us, a graip — it's dangerous to be safe around here.

TARRY He came through the hedge and made straight at me. I had to — had to hit him. (*She looks as if wondering who's to blame*) Had to. I hit him the smallest little tip you ever saw and he fell. (*Proud of himself*) For all his talk, down he fell. Weak as a cat. (*Gets carried away in his nervousness*) He wouldn't be able to pull the skin off bottled buttermilk — And that's all there was to it, the top and tail of it.

MRS FLYNN (*Rubs her wedding ring as if looking for inspiration from it*) I hope you're telling me the story right. For that man would swear a hole in a pot. And that's the kind of you anyway. (TARRY *wonders what she means, if he has or hasn't won her support*) What other man but yourself would try to steal the little grain of oats that I was keeping for the hens in the red raw summer — (*He doesn't know she knows this*) So you'd have a roughness of money yourself. That's you all over. The big fellow.

He starts to move off.

There's no use in talking to you. Your Uncle Petey all over, that the whole parish wouldn't be able to keep in drink and squandering. (*His dreams are collapsing. She is flailing in every direction*) Just like you he had nothing big about him, nothing big but talk.

She begins to think about Uncle Petey.

You'd think he was reared in a pot. Two letters in twenty years or more, and the last from a circus near Tullamore. (*Scathing*) A ringmaster! And the one before that from somewhere farther, from a place in West Africa, if you don't mind. (TARRY *has obviously never heard this*) He wrote he had nine hundred and ninety pounds and all he was asking was the other ten to buy some great big bargain — something to do with a mine. (*Reflectively*) Wasn't that a roundabout way for a man with nothing to ask for something?

Sound of a car. She goes to the window.

It's that young medical man from the town. Who the hell can be sick?

TARRY God only knows.

MRS FLYNN Must be one of the Finnegans — (*Then she realizes the implications of what she has just said*) Lord bless us and save us. (*Suddenly distracted*) Is that Larry Finnegan on the road? I'll see where he's going.

She hurries out. TARRY *waits anxiously. She returns.*

TARRY Well, what did he say?

MRS FLYNN Bad news. Bad news. He said the brother's dying.

TARRY (*Shocked*) Dying! And did you ask him what happened?

MRS FLYNN He said the less said about that the better. He said he was hurt this morning and he's very bad. He said the priest was sent for.

TARRY (*Imagining — so desperate — there's a way out of this, by laughing it off*) Was it a kick from a hen — or what?

MRS FLYNN I won't know till I go over, he said.

TARRY He's only making a show of him. He must have hurt himself when he fell on the stones, but he couldn't be too bad for I'm sure as sure that I saw him after clearing away the evidence when I left. There wasn't a track anywhere on my side when I went back this evening. (*Grasping a further piece of defence*) And didn't Eusebius say he was up with him after for the rope-twister —

But she isn't listening.

MRS FLYNN He'll swear you hit him with the slashing hook.

TARRY I'm sure there's damn all wrong with him.

MRS FLYNN Don't I know only too well that it's making out he is, but the making out is as bad as anything. There's not a whit the matter with him. (TARRY *takes comfort in this*) But what good is that to us?

TARRY The doctor ought to know.

MRS FLYNN The doctor can't tell everything.

Pause.

I was often wondering if Eusebius wasn't behind
this business. How well he wasn't more jealous at
the time of the purchase.

BRIDIE *comes in, can't wait to report.*

BRIDIE Did you hear about your pet Tarry?

MRS FLYNN What talk with you?

BRIDIE His name all over the country with Molly.

MRS FLYNN (*Springs to defence*) He never had a ha'porth to do
with the targer. How dar' you say he had! He never
laid a hand on the trollop. Have we not enough
trouble without you putting in your cutty?

Suddenly she begins to fold under it all.

That's me heart broke, night, noon and morning,
with a man that's always making little of the priest,
and won't even go to Confession. Oh, I wish, and I
more than wish, that I'd let you go to hell out of
here that time you wanted to quit the place —

But she doesn't mean this, and TARRY *knows it. She
gathers herself, goes over to the money-box, takes out a
ten shilling note, and starts putting it in an envelope.*

I'm sending that ten shilling note to the Redemp-
torists the morrow morning if the Lord spares me
and if you're not arrested. (*He starts*) And if this all
blows over you'll have to go to tell your sins. Now
in the name of God, let us kneel down and say our
prayers — for my special intention.

They kneel and begin, separate from each other in a
way different from the previous praying.

(*She leads the prayer*)
Thou O Lord wilt open my lips
And my tongue shall announce Thy praise —

    Lights fade slowly.

Scene Two

Outside, HUGHIE, CHARLIE *and* EUSEBIUS *talking, looking about, obviously little to do.*

HUGHIE Talk of the devil. There's Tarry coming over the stile.

They all watch and wait for him. TARRY *lopes on, dreaming.*

CHARLIE (*Self-consciously*) How's Tarry?

TARRY *tries to deal with the strain between* CHARLIE *and himself by being hearty.*

TARRY The best. Getting on gallant.
HUGHIE See any women lately?
TARRY None that counted anyway.
EUSEBIUS Any word about the Reilly one?
TARRY (*Uncertain*) What?
EUSEBIUS (*Explaining*) That night at the Cross?
TARRY I think that all blew over. The Mission killed it. (*Weakly*) All the same it was a damn mean thing for someone to give out my name that night (CHARLIE *moves uncomfortably*). That was a dirty lousy thing to do. (*Pointed, at* CHARLIE) I'll get that fella yet or I'll call myself a damn poor class of a man.

Awkward tension relieved by HUGHIE *looking around and off.*

HUGHIE Who's your man on the bike?

They all move to look.

EUSEBIUS (*Calls: life of the party*) You're going the wrong way!

Sudden freeze. Obviously the cyclist stops, dismounts. All four are startled. Choreography of guilty shuffling into the background. CHARLIE *and* HUGHIE *busy themselves,* EUSEBIUS *almost hides.* TARRY *is left with the situation and blame. A long pause. Then,* FR MARKEY *appears, glares at them and — worse — says nothing. Then he leaves. (It's not essential that he actually appears.* TARRY's *apology should suffice to explain.)*

TARRY (*Forced into this*) Sorry. I'm sorry, Father.
CHARLIE Oh Jaysus. Jaysus.
EUSEBIUS There'll be sport about this. There'll be sport alright. (*Bravado*) Didn't I know it was him all along.

The others disbelieve him, but aren't sure.

TARRY (*Unable to contain himself, though there are no words for his humiliation*) Jaysus, I'll — I'll —

He rushes off. The others laugh.

EUSEBIUS There's Tarry for you.
HUGHIE (*After a moment, and in response to some noise, whistling, a cough or something*) There's Patsy Meegan coming this way.
EUSEBIUS I heard he was up in Flynns' again the other evening.
CHARLIE (*Now able to study him*) He got shook.
EUSEBIUS He's near his last alright.
HUGHIE Do you think?
CHARLIE He is surely. He'll soon be given up by priest and doctor.
EUSEBIUS Yes, we'll have to pay offerings on Patsy soon.
CHARLIE The same offerings should be done away with. What must the Protestants be saying?
HUGHIE Sure the priests have to get a living anyhow.
CHARLIE (*Scornfully*) That's right, the priests have to get a living.
EUSEBIUS I'd say he's drifting out of the marriage notion.

HUGHIE   He seems to be sidling alright.

CHARLIE   He's not one bit pleased about the beating Tarry gave his cousin Joe, that's for sure.

EUSEBIUS Can't you hear her now, the oul' Flynn one. (*As Mrs Flynn*) The crooked oul' bachelor, that's all he is, a slack gelding. They're all very thick with their relations.

HUGHIE   What'll come of it anyways?

CHARLIE   Mrs Finnegan went to the Guards and they told her she'd be better off (*formally*) prosecuting. (*Important, knowing*) They said it wasn't a case for the Guards at all.

EUSEBIUS There'll be sport about this. Nothing surer.

HUGHIE   Weren't you up at the house?

CHARLIE   Yeah?

HUGHIE   (*Happily conspiratorial*) Nothing would do him the other evening only to have us sneak over by Finnegans' to see if they were rehearsing the case.

EUSEBIUS (*Joining in*) The way they always do.

CHARLIE   (*A well-known fact, evidently*) Every time.

EUSEBIUS Sure it's as good as a play. Maybe better.

HUGHIE   Whisht. Here's Patsy now.

> PATSY *comes on. As they greet him, they make excessive efforts to disguise the fact they've been talking about him.*

CHARLIE   Grand evening.

HUGHIE   (*As if this is addressed to him*) Powerful.

PATSY   That's the way.

EUSEBIUS You were up at the house —

> PATSY *looks as if 'which'? Flynns'? Finnegans'? What's* EUSEBIUS *getting at? General distrust.* EUSEBIUS *begins to pamper him.*

That was woeful carry-on at Finnegans'. Will it go to the Law? I'd say you've a damn strong case. A damn strong case.

74

PATSY (*Falling for this*) Would you think?

EUSEBIUS I'm sure and certain.

> *They slip into a re-enactment of what* EUSEBIUS *and* HUGHIE *must have witnessed.*

Sure Joe would only have to say (*as Joe, giving evidence*) I was coming quietly down me drills of potatoes to see if they were blighted when I saw the defendant on *my* side of the hedge in a fighting attitude. He had a slash-hook in his hand.

HUGHIE (*As solicitor*) Mr Finnegan, you were afraid of the defendant, no doubt —

> PATSY *is thrown by the accuracy of their version.*

EUSEBIUS (*As Joe*) I was terrified of him, your Honour; he's a very peculiar class of a man.

HUGHIE (*As solicitor*) You thought he was about to attack you?

EUSEBIUS (*As Joe*) I did. I was sure and certain.

HUGHIE (*As solicitor*) You said nothing to anger him?

> PATSY *still puzzled, how could they know?*

EUSEBIUS (*As Joe*) I never opened my mouth.

HUGHIE (*As solicitor*) He then attacked you and you tried to defend yourself?

EUSEBIUS (*As Joe*) I did the best I could.

HUGHIE (*As solicitor*) Flynn is a much bigger man than you?

EUSEBIUS (*As Joe*) He's a big bad man; I'd bate the breed of him in any kind of a fair fight — I'd throw the breed of him over that bleddy ditch before my breakfast.

> PATSY, *despite his caution, steps in with the advice that must have been given at the real 'rehearsal'.*

PATSY If you said a thing like that you'd be bet before you started.

The scene breaks up.

CHARLIE (*Not wishing to let the fun end*) We'd better try Flynn in the box while we're at it.

EUSEBIUS Come on, Patsy. You be Tarry.

HUGHIE Get in the box.

They move PATSY *formally to a spot which is now the 'witness-box'.*

PATSY I'm ready.

Now PATSY *— absurd, but with a venemous delight — becomes Tarry.*

HUGHIE (*As solicitor*) Your mother bought a farm, is that the case?

PATSY (*As Tarry*) I admit she bought a farm.

HUGHIE (*As solicitor*) And she bought it in a way that's known as grabbing a farm, isn't that so?

PATSY (*As Tarry, scratches his head, gazes away*) She gave the full value for it, if I know anything.

HUGHIE (*As solicitor*) Would it be any harm to ask you where she got the money to pay for it?

PATSY (*As Tarry, taking offence at the mention of money, refuses to answer, looks further away, as Tarry might. The others, relishing his act*) There's a great beauty in stones and weeds —

The others all laughter, PATSY *laughing himself. The sweetness of revenge. Suddenly* TARRY *comes on, dragging the sprayer awkwardly. He has clearly seen some of the mockery.*

TARRY (*Rage, to no one in particular*) You're a lousy bastard.

Everyone caught off guard. No one knows where to look. PATSY *is especially unable for this.*

EUSEBIUS Sure it's only a bit of a laugh. Don't you know right well they haven't a case at all?

> PATSY's *confusion.* TARRY *is not appeased.* CHARLIE *risks changing the subject in the hope* TARRY *hasn't seen it all.*

CHARLIE That Shaw's a hard man. (*The others smile, grasping his drift before* TARRY *does*)

TARRY (*Off guard, doesn't catch the reference*) What? What's that you're saying?

CHARLIE Shaw — (*But now not so sure of himself*) You know, the writer. Shaw?

TARRY Give over. Quit!

EUSEBIUS (*Rallying to stand by* CHARLIE *and pick further at* TARRY — *best defence is attack* — *so many resentments are being aired*) Still, you're a desperate man to be making little of the priests like that.

HUGHIE (*Joining in,* PATSY *conspicuously silent*) We're all Catholics, aren't we?

TARRY I don't know so much about that anymore. Some of us are doubtful.

> HUGHIE *doesn't quite understand what's going on; as ever, he's along for the ride.*

CHARLIE (*Sensing an opening, wanting to settle scores*) Oh, I see, you don't believe in religion now —

TARRY (*Withering look*) No, but *you* do, don't you?

> CHARLIE *is deflated by what this could mean by the way* TARRY *says it. The others are no longer supporting. He's alone, but rallies.*

CHARLIE (*To* HUGHIE) Come on, we'll away. There's no more here.

> EUSEBIUS *makes to go with them.* PATSY *is abandoned to a look from* TARRY *who has won some terribly small*

victory. PATSY *looks old as he shuffles off.* TARRY, *alone a long while.* MRS FLYNN *comes on, with a bottle of milk, corked with paper.*

MRS FLYNN   What's all the commotion? Where's that crowd gone?

She senses a problem, and knows its kind. She and TARRY *know they've been isolated further. Throughout what follows we understand all that goes without saying.*

It's no wonder I do be telling you to mind your things with the class of people that's on the go in this country.

TARRY   Patsy will hardly come back for Bridie.

MRS FLYNN   No loss. (*Complete volte face*) Aggie was telling one of the priests in the Mission and he said she'd be mad to have anything to do with him. He said that it would be a sin for a young girl to marry the man. And do you know, I kind of think he's right. Yes, there's something unnatural about that man. I heard Eusebius talking about his ways. I wouldn't like to eat the eggs his hens lay.

TARRY, *though he's not sure what she means, inclines to agree.*

Lord, I hope they make a fist of their new place.

TARRY   What's that you're saying?

MRS FLYNN   I'm getting on in years, Tarry. (*For a moment she's vulnerable, a change which strikes* TARRY *with some force*) If Bridie and Aggie were settled I'd die in peace.

TARRY   What are you talking about at all?

MRS FLYNN   They're thinking of starting an eating-house in the town. A good stand is not to be laughed at. And they'd have a better chance of getting a man that way. Since she went to the factory May Tallon has scores of young fellas after her — And even if they are barefooted gossuns, at least they're young hardy chaps. If you happen to meet one of the Finnegans up the road don't say one word. Last Saturday when I was at my Confession I mentioned the trouble to Father Markey and he said them and Christians differ and that he was going to talk to them one of these days. We're having trouble with the Finnegans, says I. Very hot-tempered people, said he, very hot-tempered. There's not one of the priests that wouldn't put his hands beneath my feet. But *you* haven't the wit of a two-year-old child, always trying to belittle the people who'd do you a good turn. You're on the right side of Father Markey's book now — (TARRY *shuffles awkwardly. She doesn't know about the latest incident on the laneway, but she'll hear*) — so take care to keep it so. You should always put yourself over big with the priests. You'd never know when you'd want one of them to do you a good turn. (*Muses*) Terrible the changes that's taking place, Tarry.

He nods in agreement. They are united in disappointments.

TARRY Still, we mightn't worry.

MRS FLYNN *looks as if to say, How so?*

When I went to town for the spraying stuff —
MRS FLYNN I suppose the clerks in Maganns were surprised you weren't in jail —
TARRY Anyway, who came up to the shop from the public house end only Jack Smith the Blacksmith — he was in for the 'cure' — and, said he, if you want a witness to stand for you, I'll not hesitate. But you hardly saw what happened, says I. Don't mind about that, said he. Only letting on to be hurted, that's all, you don't worry, sham-shiting behind the hedge he is. Are you sure of that, Jack? said I.

Positive, I'm positive, said he.

MRS FLYNN And what did you tell him?

TARRY Sure I stood him a drink.

MRS FLYNN Good man. That's why I like you to have money in your pocket. Not to be smoking it and wasting it.

TARRY picks up the sprayer. MRS FLYNN hands him the bottle of milk. A moment of tenderness, her thoughtfulness.

I don't want you to be stooping down to drink out of that well; I do be afraid you'll fall in one fine day.

They look at each other — close to a loving look.

Scene Three

BRIDIE *and* TARRY. *Kitchen. Sound of the gate opening.* TARRY *goes out. Greeting, small talk, farewells overheard.* TARRY *returns with a letter. He opens it quickly and reads it.* MRS FLYNN *comes in from outside.* TARRY *hides the letter, watched by* BRIDIE.

MRS FLYNN   You got a letter?

TARRY   Who said I got a letter?

MRS FLYNN   Isn't there a postman going back the road? Must be in Cassidys' he was. I thought it might be that Uncle Petey of yours who was threatening to come back to lie up on us — as if we weren't bad enough already. Come to think of it it's about time we heard from that solicitor about the new farm. One of these days I'll go myself and find out what's keeping him with that deed. (*At the door, as she goes out*) I never liked the look of that man even if he is Father Markey's cousin.

Exits.

BRIDIE   Well?

TARRY   Well, what?

BRIDIE   What's in the letter?

TARRY   (*Needing to share its news*) There appears to be — (*he takes out the letter and refers to it*) — some trouble (*formally, quoting*) over the boundaries of the holding. Two fields appear now not to be included in the purchased property. And he's asking if we'd call at his office.

MRS FLYNN comes back in, with AGGIE, and sees him folding and putting away the letter. Her look demands an answer. He is caught so obviously it doesn't warrant a comment.

(*To his mother*) It's from Daly. The solicitor. It only

says he'd like to see one of us whenever we happened to be in the town. There doesn't appear to be any hurry on him — (*limply*) so far as I can see.

MRS FLYNN And why is it we haven't the deed complete by this? If I could depend on you I wouldn't care, but I can't trust you as far as I'd throw you. (*To* BRIDIE, *sharply, all business*) Bridie, you, you'll go to see him. Get yourself ready.

BRIDIE *goes upstairs.*

TARRY Didn't I tell you I'd go on the bicycle and see him? When I went the first time, I should go the second. What'll he think at all? How many times did I say I'd go to see him?

MRS FLYNN She'll tell him all I tell her to say. The whole bill of the races. Of course she'll have to report the row our wonderful man here had with that savage, Joe Finnegan.

TARRY *looks insulted.*

If he hasn't heard all about it already, that is.

TARRY *storms towards the door, looks out.*

TARRY Who took them calves down?

MRS FLYNN Aggie and I brought them down till things are settled.

TARRY That's just giving in.

AGGIE And met Eusebius going up the road with one-two-three-four-five cattle. That's the man, says she (*Mrs Flynn*), when she saw them, that'd make a spoon or spoil a horn.
You gave a brave penny for them, says she.
How much would you think? says he.
Did you give ten a-piece?
I did, and the rest.

And they're worth every penny, says she. When they get a bit of grass, they'll be wonderful animals. There's no doubt we're only in the ha'penny place with you, Eusebius.

MRS FLYNN (*Cuts in*) I wouldn't let them about the place. Five of as hungry a cattle as ever I saw. Must have bought them from some of the long-nosed scutch-grass farmers of Monaghan. (*To* TARRY) Why don't you take pattern by Eusebius? The song the black-bird sang to Paddy McNamee is the truest song ever sung.

BRIDIE *comes in, dressed and made up.*

Have it, said he, or do without.

MRS FLYNN *and* BRIDIE *go out the door for* BRIDIE's *'briefing'.* TARRY *and* AGGIE *uncomfortable together. What can they say? She goes out before* MRS FLYNN *returns.* TARRY *waits guiltily.*

MRS FLYNN Don't fret.
TARRY Will it be alright?
MRS FLYNN Sure it has to be.

TARRY *looks doubtful.*

When these ones are away — give the men their fill and that's all they want — you'll have a free house here in no time.

TARRY's *unease as she conjures his future again.* MRS FLYNN's *thoughts begin to wander.*

I think you'll have rain. This corn on my wee toe is at me again. I wonder would you get the razor blade and pare it for me?

He starts to do this.

Easy now, and don't draw blood. Easy now. We'll put a sprag in Finnegan's wheel over the case. And if I'm not too contented over the solicitor, I'll get Father Markey to see about it. Please God it'll all come out alright.

There is an intimacy now between them.

Oh yes, it's you that could have the good time here. When you're the independent man. You made a great job of that corn, Tarry, a great job. (*Pause*) You know I wouldn't prevent you bringing in a woman here. (TARRY's *surprise*) And you know I wouldn't be too stiff about money either (*higher surprise*). Sure there's no one in the parish cares less for money than I do or would more like to see you with your pockets full when you went out (TARRY *incredulous by now*) — so long as you wouldn't spend it. This house'll be empty shortly and in here they'll never show their noses again. Yes, it's you that could tell them all to kiss your —

She checks herself, as if such language ill-fits a woman of her new standing.

Scene Four

Sunday evening. Dance scene. Outside — by building. Night time. Noise of concert/dance. Hammed up recitation of verse, off-stage.

> (*Great melodrama*)
> If any born of kindlier blood
> Should ask what maiden lies below
> Say only this: A tender bud,
> That tried to blossom in the snow,
> Lies withered where the violets grow.

> *Sounds mid-scene of concert ending, and music/ dancing beginning.* TARRY *shuffling about.* EUSEBIUS *comes on singing, with a bucket of water, busy helping.*

EUSEBIUS It wasn't the men from Shercock
Or the men from Ballybay
But the dalin' (*dealing*) men from Crossmaglen —

TARRY (*Calls*) Eusebius. Here.

EUSEBIUS (*When he sees* TARRY, *speaks the last line of 'song'*) Put whiskey in me tay.

TARRY Eusebius?

EUSEBIUS Ah, Tarry. There you are. Are you not going in?

TARRY (*Feigning disinterest*) I might and I mightn't. (*Then, focussed*) I wonder could you lend us fourpence till the morrow?

EUSEBIUS Honest to Christ, Tarry. I can't. I'm riding on the rims myself. I haven't a penny on me. I gave the last ha'penny I had for a packet of fags.

TARRY Ah, go on. It's not much to ask —

EUSEBIUS Throw them the two-and-two, it's good enough for them.

TARRY Only give them the chance to laugh at me. You couldn't trust Charlie not to make a show of me.

EUSEBIUS If I had it I'd give it to you, Tarry, you know that.

TARRY (*Bitterly*) Oh, I do. I do surely. (*Almost to himself*) Fourpence isn't much when you have it. But when you haven't it's as hard got as four pounds. You don't happen to know who's performing —

EUSEBIUS Don't you know well, the usual — all the educated people: the schoolmaster, the stationmaster and the postman. That's what you might call the right singer. You know, you want a bit of education to go up on a stage.

TARRY And what's with the buckets?

EUSEBIUS Didn't I tell you that Father Markey asked me three weeks ago, the day I was coming from Confession (*TARRY's surprise*), if I'd help to make the tay for all the swanks?

He sees TARRY *is jealous of his 'importance'.*

TARRY And why the hell didn't you tell a fella? You're too bleddy mean.

EUSEBIUS If you had to mention it to me at the time, I could have you with me on the job —

TARRY (*Enraged*) Who the hell said I wanted the job?

EUSEBIUS There you are now.

Pause.

(*Rubbing it in*) There's a band in there that's damn good. And why wouldn't it be — and them after coming all the way from Clones? Every man jack of that band gets a pound and a kick for his night.

TARRY (*Envious*) A week's wages. Easy earned.

EUSEBIUS (*Salt in the wound*) It's a shame you'd need a ticket for the dance at the end of the concert.

TARRY's case is lost.

(*Busy*) These swanks drink the devil's amount of tay.

TARRY (*In desperation*) Who's inside?

EUSEBIUS All the boys.

TARRY But what women?

EUSEBIUS The usual. Just the usual crowd.

TARRY Isn't that a dread, a holy dread!

EUSEBIUS A holy dread is right. Here, take one of these cans and you can snaffle your way in.

TARRY (*Tempted, but condemned to remain outside*) I wouldn't chance it. Father Markey's there and he'd only go for me.

EUSEBIUS He'll be away off with the money soon and you can get in when he's gone. Here, take one of these (*cans*).

> TARRY *hesitates an age.*

(*Gives up*) Whatever you think yourself. I'll be back anyway.

> *He exits.* TARRY *waits, paces up and down. Tries to look in.* EUSEBIUS *returns without the cans/buckets.*

TARRY (*Eager for news*) How's it going on?

EUSEBIUS A few nice bulling heifers in there, right enough.

TARRY But Mary Reilly. Who's Mary with? Did she get much of a show?

EUSEBIUS I don't think she waited for the dance at all. (*Though he knows*) Why?

> TARRY *is confused, tries to be casual.*

TARRY Oh, nothing.

EUSEBIUS A lot of the swanks didn't wait, you know.

TARRY Still, if I had that fourpence —

EUSEBIUS (*Easy for him to say*) Hardly worth your while now.

TARRY (*Suddenly resolute*) I'm thinking of chucking the whole damn thing.

EUSEBIUS (*Not fully attentive*) Chucking what?

TARRY Drumnay. Drumnay, Dargan, the whole place.

EUSEBIUS You are in me arse.

TARRY I am. And then you can have all the women to yourself. And all the land. I don't give a tuppenny damn for any of it.

87

They both know he doesn't mean this. EUSEBIUS *changes the subject.*

EUSEBIUS I saw a friend of yours in Longford town the other day. An uncle of yours, he said he was.

> TARRY *registers this, but has more pressing concerns. He slinks off.* EUSEBIUS *goes back in. A while later — watched by* TARRY *who has stayed to check —* EUSEBIUS *comes out, with* MARY. *She looks around, as if looking for someone. Then* EUSEBIUS *helps her put on her coat, and they go off together.* TARRY *emerges to stand alone. His world has collapsed.*

End of scene.

Scene Five

Kitchen. BRIDIE, *with* TARRY *flicking through the paper, restlessly.*

MRS FLYNN (*Off, cries in a broken voice*) Tarry, Tarry, Tarry. Are you in or are you out?

> TARRY *withdraws.* MRS FLYNN *comes in, looks around, sees* BRIDIE *and notices Aggie's absence.*

Where's that one?
BRIDIE Out.
MRS FLYNN Out where?

> BRIDIE *shrugs.*

And where's that fella? (*Calls*) Tarry!
TARRY (*Knowing she's heard something*) I'm here.

> TARRY *re-enters.*

MRS FLYNN The Lord save us and bless us, but it's a sudden world.
TARRY (*Going to console her*) What's the matter, Mother?
MRS FLYNN What in the wide earthly world are we to do at all? First this one here (BRIDIE) comes back from the town saying there's no trade in the eating-house. And all their notions. How often I said it: how would you make ends meet in a town without a railway line? Isn't there the buses, said they? Oh they knew it all, themselves and you and your Uncle — (*she restrains herself from saying 'Petey'*). I'll say no more. And now this.
TARRY What else is the matter?
MRS FLYNN God! Oh God! Oh God! Isn't it all suffering and sorrow? And you told me that you saw the map and knew everything!
TARRY What map? (*But he knows*)

MRS FLYNN What map! What's the matter! Everything's the matter. Everything. I was better dead and in the boneyard than have to put up with this. Oh it's me that's to be pitied if ever a woman was to be pitied.

TARRY Pull yourself together. Is it over Carlins'?

MRS FLYNN Is it over Carlins'? Is it over Carlins'! Lord, Oh Lord. Better dead and in the boneyard. A thousand times better.

> AGGIE *comes in, dressed in good, town/going away clothes, with a small suitcase.*

AGGIE What's going on? Is Tarry alright?

> *She sees that he is.*

I heard he was near killed. Will somebody tell me what's going on? Is it true what they're saying?

MRS FLYNN Who?

BRIDIE (*Almost simultaneously*) What?

MRS FLYNN (*Taking control*) Who's saying what?

> TARRY *is conspicuously quiet, listening intently.*

BRIDIE It's only what Eusebius was saying, and Charlie Trainor —

> MRS FLYNN *and* TARRY *look as if to say, Go on.*

They were saying Jemmy Carlin went rushing at Tarry up at our new farm with a rusty graip like — (*she's trying to remember the word*) like a — javelin.

TARRY The same man'd go through you for a shortcut.

AGGIE (*Continuing*) And bawling at him 'Trespassers will be — (*she is trying to remember the word*) perse-cuted'. And Charlie was saying, Jemmy said 'I'll drive this graip through you, you grabber, if you step a foot inside me fields'. 'Trespassers'? *His* fields? (*She is trying to make sense of it all*)

MRS FLYNN (*To* TARRY) Well?

> TARRY *evidently decides to come clean, moves forward*
> *to report.*

TARRY Didn't we buy them fields off you, says I, and gave
a fair price for them? Buy my good fields? said he.
You couldn't buy my good fields. You bought the
brother's farm, but you didn't buy mine. By God,
but you didn't buy mine. (*He can no longer pretend*
this isn't a disaster) And I may as well tell you, he said,
if your cattle put their noses into one of those two
good fields of mine, they'll calve before their time.

MRS FLYNN How often did I tell you to buy a thing with your
two eyes open? (TARRY'*s surprise*) But what's the
use in talking? (*Defeated, to* AGGIE, *noticing her dress,*
the case, etc.) And where were you anyway?

AGGIE Waiting.

MRS FLYNN What do you mean 'waiting'?

AGGIE Waiting. (*Resigned*) I was waiting for Tommy.

MRS FLYNN (*With no surprise*) And he didn't show.

AGGIE No.

BRIDIE And I thought he was mad keen.

MRS FLYNN Ah, them Quinns. I wouldn't even it to them.
They're all the one. You couldn't be up to them.

AGGIE (*Very quietly*) I suppose he got what he wanted.

> *The grim likelihood seeps in.* BRIDIE *moves to console*
> *her sister in the one gesture of comfort we see, which*
> MRS FLYNN *promptly disrupts.*

MRS FLYNN Lord, Oh Lord! Better dead and in the boneyard.
A thousand times better.

> *She goes into herself by the fire.* BRIDIE *and* AGGIE
> *try to escape the force of her grief.*

BRIDIE (*To* TARRY) Come away over here and let the temper
wear off.

AGGIE   It's the only cure. Time's the cure for anything.

> *They withdraw and talk quietly, checking from time to time on their mother.*

BRIDIE (*Suddenly, and almost surprised herself*) You know the parish of Dargan, and the people in it, it's no place for a civilized man or woman. A girl was better sell herself on the streets of a city.

TARRY   (*Not knowing what to make of the revelation, he changes the subject to one he'd prefer. He has lost Mary. He turns to another prospect*) What do you think about the Molly one?

BRIDIE (*Quietly*) What the hell about her! Why the hell should you care — if you'd nothing to do with her, and even if you had, for that matter.

> TARRY *is troubled. They look over towards their mother.*

AGGIE   She's slowing down a bit now.

BRIDIE Don't say a word.

TARRY   Not one.

> *They move towards* MRS FLYNN. TARRY *takes a nip of raisin bread from the dresser.* AGGIE *grins her disapproval.* TARRY *drinks from the milk jug.*

BRIDIE (*Whispers*) You'll start her off again.

TARRY   Wait. You know what you were saying about this place — ?

BRIDIE What?

TARRY   About it not being right for the likes of us?

BRIDIE Well?

TARRY   Well, I was often thinking the same thing myself.

> *They look at each other in a new recognition.*

(*Quietly, kindly*) Leave us alone. I'll talk to her.

BRIDIE *and* AGGIE *exit. There's an awkward silence.* MRS FLYNN *has been muttering parts of the Rosary. Suddenly she straightens and listens.* TARRY *listens, too. A motor car coming up the lane, a slow ominous purr.* MRS FLYNN *sits up, sticks her feet in her shoes. They wait anxiously to see if the car will pass their house. Next they hear the rattle of the gate and a man's voice guiding the driver to turn.*

MRS FLYNN   Father, Son and Holy Ghost. Did something happen to one of ours in Shercock? One trouble never comes alone.

BRIDIE *and* AGGIE *return.* TARRY *runs to the door.* MRS FLYNN *is frozen to the tiles of the hearth praying 'Father, Son and Holy Ghost. God protect everybody's rearing.'*

VOICE   (*Loud, affable, to* TARRY) Are you the man I heard so much about from your mother whenever she took the notion of answering my letters?

MRS FLYNN   (*Vicious whispers*) Bad luck to him to hell and out the other side, who is it but Uncle Petey!

UNCLE PETEY *appears, well enough dressed, but obviously disreputable. What the world thinks of him doesn't seem to matter. He moves towards his sister,* MRS FLYNN. *Though he's obviously been away, he still has traces of a Cavan accent.*

PETEY   How are you, Mary? (*Takes a good look at her*) My God, but you aged a lot, Mary.

MRS FLYNN   (*As if relieved the news wasn't worse*) Hang his coat on the back of the door, Bridie.

MRS FLYNN *herself takes his suitcase, and weighs it furtively, then leaves it aside. Sound of horn outside. Looks. An awkward silence.*

PETEY Mary, would you ever go out and pay that driver
the few shillings he's owed? I have no small change
on me.

> MRS FLYNN, *knowing full well, goes out.* TARRY
> *suggests disappointment, apprehending that his uncle*
> *has no money, money being the currency of success.*
> MRS FLYNN *returns, and ushers the sisters upstairs*
> *to bed. As she follows she says to them*

MRS FLYNN The right rodney if ever there was one. Not a thing
in the suitcase except a lock of oul' rags — and a
couple of books very likely.

> TARRY, *alone with* PETEY, *is unsure what to do.*

PETEY So this is the farm? Doesn't it look very small?

TARRY (*Trying to make the best of it*) It's not so bad, and bad
beats worse — as the man said.

PETEY Living in the country is a hard old station. Crooked
lanes and little lumpy hills.

TARRY Ah now.

PETEY Aaaragh, land be damned! What's in land anyways? A bite to eat — and a bad bite at that. The
man that would stay on land is a compound eejit.

TARRY (*Taking this nearly personally*) I wouldn't say that.

PETEY A dead loss. Bounded by the whitethorn hedges,
sure what would you know of the world?

TARRY (*Defensively, and almost surprising himself*) Sometimes
when the sun comes through a gap you'd know
God the Father in a tree.

PETEY (*Unsure of what to make of this, nods towards the door*)
Is Molly still living yonder? (*Whether* PETEY *knows*
more than he's saying is hard to tell)

TARRY (*Pleased by this subject*) Oh aye, she is.

PETEY I knew her well. A hot piece. She married an oul'
fella, I heard.

TARRY He died two years after.

PETEY Any family?

TARRY One daughter is all she has. She's Molly, too. They say there's something wrong with her.

PETEY Ah, a trout in the well! These things do be in it, Tarry. And worse can happen a woman.

TARRY They're putting it out that I had something to do with the younger one, (*formal*) but I may as well tell you I hadn't.

PETEY *is hardly listening.*

PETEY (*Seriously*) What do you want to do about that? What do you really want?

TARRY (*Honestly*) I don't know.

PETEY My advice is this — and I always acted on it — do whatever pleases you.

TARRY *is taking in the advice.*

I remember it well. Fifty years ago. I wed potatoes in that longish field by Carlins' — and the devil's rotten spuds they were. What a life! How do you bear it, Tarry?

TARRY *is about to defend it.*

TARRY (*Resigned, wavering*) I don't know.

PETEY It's alright and fine in its own way, but it will get you nowhere. There's no necessity to live in this sort of a place, is there? The best way to love a place like this is from a distance. (*Pause. Sympathetic*) And the same applies to the women of it.

PETEY *flits in and out of subjects.*

How's oul' Joe Finnegan? He was the second greatest blackguard I ever met, and I like him for it. Poor Joe Finnegan.

TARRY There was a fierce quarrel a time ago. He'll not speak to us now.

95

PETEY (*Dismissively*) Is it Joe Finnegan? Don't be foolish. I knew his wife, too. Many's the coort I had with her.

TARRY (*Surprised*) With Maggie? (*Then, seriously*) But what did you think of Joe? Really?

PETEY (*Displaying vicious power, and his true self*) That fella was always afraid of me. I could make him run into a rat hole. (*Pause. He changes tone*) Do you know, Tarry, it often occurred to me that we love most what makes us most miserable. In my opinion the damned are damned because they enjoy being damned. You know, you could do worse than leave Drumnay with me.

> TARRY *torn, but resisting.*

TARRY It's not as if I haven't thought about it.

PETEY I may not have a fortune of money. But I have some influence. I could get you a job and I could get you what's better, a living! It's not what you make but what you spend that makes you rich. I often wondered if I'd stay — I know your mother would like me to (TARRY's *raised eyes*) — but there's a man I know with a car calling for me in a while.

TARRY (*Flustered*) But what will my mother say? How will she carry on without me?

PETEY If you were dead you'd be done without.

TARRY (*Confused*) I love this place, the dunghill and the muddy haggard and the gaps —

PETEY Haven't you all these things in your mind, the best place for them? If they're as beautiful as you imagine you can take them with you. Anyway, isn't life the same anywhere?

> TARRY *fears this may be true. His resolve hardens, then weakens.*

TARRY What about money?

PETEY Is there any around? Is there any anywhere in the house?

He gets up and starts looking around. TARRY *suddenly surrenders to* PETEY's *intention and, while* PETEY *makes distracting noise, prises open a trunk and takes out, one by one, four pound notes.*

PETEY Any more in it?
TARRY Five.
PETEY Well get it, we might be short-taken on the road.

TARRY starts gathering some bits and pieces, goes out and returns quickly wearing a suit/coat. MRS FLYNN *reappears.*

MRS FLYNN Father, Son and Holy Ghost, where are you going in the good suit?
TARRY *(Lamely)* As far as the village.
MRS FLYNN And with the good suit?

She eyes him with annoyance, then suddenly her eyes flash in scalded grief.

(To TARRY, *as if this is his way of betraying her)* You were never rightly settled here. You were always looking for something.

She glares at PETEY, *and sits. Her lips begin to move in prayer. Then, in a slow whisper*

MRS FLYNN God help me and every mother.
TARRY *(Uncertain, to* PETEY *)* How will she carry on? How?
PETEY *(Dispassionately)* Women never have got full credit for their bravery. They sacrifice everything to life. Come on, we'll wait for the car by the door.

He leads TARRY *towards the door.* MRS FLYNN *resumes her crouched position at the fire, mumbling prayers. Alone in the world.* BRIDIE *and* AGGIE *re-enter. The three women resume abandoned positions at the hearth. Spotlight on* TARRY *and* PETEY.

PETEY Shut your eyes and you'll see it all better. Tell me, is Father Markey still in Dargan?

TARRY (*Lifelessly*) He is.

PETEY Terrible pity of that poor man. Living here at the back of God's speed. I met the Pope once and if I'd have thought of it I'd have put in a good word for him.

TARRY (*Warming to the adventure, trying to be brave*) You met the Pope?

PETEY Yes, the only thing a man could do in a place like this is drink himself to death. I could have fixed him up if I'd only thought of it.

TARRY You met the Pope?

PETEY Oh yes. (*He dares a flourish*) Knew him rather well actually —

> *Ends. Slowly, then gradually into music and song, filling the theatre.*

On a quiet street where old ghosts meet
    I see her walking now
Away from me so hurriedly
    my reason must allow
That I had wooed not as I should
    a creature made of clay —
When the angel woos the clay he'd lose
    his wings at the dawn of day.

An Afterword

This adaptation of Patrick Kavanagh's *Tarry Flynn* was a project I took on in the spring of 1994 during my term as Writer Fellow in the School of English at Trinity College, Dublin. It was a way of re-reading a novel, first published in 1948, by a poet whose works had continued to weave their spells since I read them closely for the first time when I was an undergraduate at the same university more than twenty years earlier. It was, also, a way of re-viewing a world which I'd encountered growing up on my uncle's farm in Carnaross, near Kells, in County Meath, and with which I remained intimate through the works and days of my neighbours in and around Loughcrew, a few miles to the west of my home place, where I have lived for thirty years.

At that time I was also engaged as agent of the literary estate of Patrick Kavanagh. In 1986, the poet's widow, Katherine, asked for my advice and help. She was then receiving paltry royalties from her husband's work and scant recognition that she was entitled to them. She had been, essentially, bullied out of the record. In the years that I worked as her representative and, after her death, as the agent of the Trustees nominated in her will, I investigated and asserted her legal rights and secured her proper dues. In the course of her last three years I met or talked with her three or four times a month in her home in Rathgar and, finally, on 4 August 1989, two weeks before her death, in a private nursing home in Santry. I learned much from her about the years she spent with Patrick. On 19 August 1989 I helped to dig her grave in Inniskeen, County Monaghan.

Though I never knew Patrick Kavanagh — I was sixteen when he died — it was a family friend of ours, Doctor Irene Creedon from Carrickmacross, who tended him at the onset of his final illness. As much as anything I hoped to restore Katherine's self-esteem. When the courts found in her favour and contracts were in place, I had attained my goal. Now her Trustees, through the Jonathan Williams Agency, exercise the rights in Patrick Kavanagh's writings, and I thank them for their permission to publish in this version excerpts from the novel and to quote from the poems and other prose.

The production of *Tarry Flynn*, and its simultaneous publication, result from a seemingly casual enquiry in a letter from one George B Miller to The Gallery Press about the performing rights in another play on the Gallery list. He wrote from his theatre company in Pennsylvania: 'We know Gallery Press, and Fallon as a poet, but has Peter written plays or stories?' My answer was no — and yes. Time to dust down this script, I thought, to see if it might interest him. I was conscious, of course, that the Ireland it depicted had suffered seismic changes: the economic excesses of the last decade — along with shifting attitudes in, and to, the Church, and an ever-widening urban/rural division — had despatched its particular kind of poverty and hungers to a suddenly historical past.

But Kavanagh's vision, and version of a life, are founded in enduring verities. There is more than a little truth in his famous and characteristically extravagant claim in *Self-Portrait* (1964) that the novel is 'not only the best but the only authentic account of life as it was lived in Ireland' up to that point in the twentieth century.

To Kate Scuffle and George B Miller I give thanks for that seemingly innocent question and for their enthusiastic commitment to this work. I dedicate the edition to the memories of Katherine Kavanagh and of my Uncle Peter. One clear day in 1957, the day we arrived to stay permanently in Ireland, he took this then five-year-old boy by the hand and had me 'help' him with a lambing. On that February afternoon he put before me what has turned out to be a crucial, sustaining part of my life.

Peter Fallon
August 2004